25 Assertions about Leader Role & Effectiveness

By

Richard C. Lumb, Ph.D.

Copyright © 2014. Richard C. Lumb, Wilton, Maine, PSPP&R, LLC.
First published in 2014 by CreateSpace Independent Publishing Platform. ISBN-10: 1500752312. ISBN-13: 978-1500752316.

Index
Content List.

Preface.

Chapters – Leader Assertions.

---

[1]

http://faculty.weber.edu/molpin/healthclasses/1110/bookchapters/selfassessmentchapter.htm

Twenty Five Leader Assertions

1. Leaders place the organization first and personal interest second.

2. Leaders are able to leverage employee and organizational outcomes versus the more common hierarchal and bureaucratic model.

3. Leaders continually perfect their role and responsibilities.

4. Leaders leverage resources and relationships to achieve success.

5. Leaders look beyond day-to-day activities and incorporate a future focus.

6. Leaders manage immediate and short-term needs while anticipating change, growth and future direction.

7. Leaders continually scan internal and external environments, adjust plans, manage resources, and direct employees to fulfill the mission efficiently and effectively.

8. Leaders are visionary with regard to their organization's mission and purpose.

9. Leaders navigate cultures and motivate people.

10. Leaders provide honest feedback.

11. Leaders guide people in doing things right and correcting unacceptable performance and attitudes.

12. Leaders assist people to examine their future and assist them with career development.

13. Leaders stretch to the positive and recognize that mistakes occur. They help individuals overcome future error.

14. Leaders provide a blend of balance and good management.

15. Leaders look after their people. They do not shy away from high expectations and hold people accountable to the mission. They devote time and energy to grow their subordinates.

16. Leaders are proactive and provide time mentoring others to effect positive change.

17. Leaders align people to future jobs preparing them for new positions and responsibilities.

18. Leaders evaluate and provide meaningful performance appraisal.

19. Leaders help employees understand the organization's mission and goals and guide them in the delivery of services.

20. Leaders communicate openly with people.

21. Leaders insist on resilient ethical and moral behavior.

22. Leaders personally adhere to a strong code of conduct and demand it of others in the organization.

23. Leaders make sound decisions based on the acquisition of full information and careful analysis.

24. Leaders encourage innovation and best practices.

25. Leaders are aware of the need for self-development and personal growth.

> # Be the Leader
> # You Were Meant To Be

Successful organizations consistently adhere to achieving their mission and goals while insuring that employee efforts are directed in their fulfillment[1].

Introduction

Leadership is critical to well-run organizations, groups, volunteers, special projects and all manner of activity that affects others and where direction, attention to detail and oversight are critical to achieving mission, vision, values, goals, objectives and desired outcomes.

The word leadership is bantered about and used liberally as a panacea to good management, getting people to perform their duties, and as the key to a well-run organization. Perhaps that is true but when the word itself is used without examination of how it is being applied or if it applies to the situation at hand, we occasionally encounter a dilemma. People interpret the word leadership without grounding it into something tangible and as such it can mean anything that we want it too simply by saying it. That is contentious to say the least for unless we are able to apply meaning to performance, all else is meaningless.

To help differentiate meaning and to break down the concept leader and leadership, we need to determine the operative applications to real examples. How do leaders function with others in a variety of environments and situations? Are there rules or principles that must be followed and carefully monitored? What influences can change outcomes and how do we address them? Do leaders actually make a difference or are the rules of procedure more prominent in achieving outcomes?

Considering these questions, it was thought that if individuals used a set of rules, general assertions about aspects of work and life, outcomes were likely to be achieved. The following assertions reflect leader competence and effectiveness in guiding employee achievement of the organization's mission and delivery of services. The twenty-five assertions are provided as the foundation of excellent supervision and management, a product of individual skills, knowledge, abilities and experience. Assertions by their very nature do not provide a list of steps that should be followed. Assertions are statements that declare potential and affirmation and if used situationally are conducive to successful outcome.

Performance implication

Occasional performance drift occurs and the mission of the agency may become blurred. During the period of diverted focus, effectiveness and efficiency suffer and new habits are formed that over time become harmful to intended outcomes. A lessening of commitment emerges from both the organization and its employees due to numerous side influences. Some of them include:

- Job change and turnover
- Diminished communications
- Retention of a top-down mentality
- Simmering adversity and/or anger
- High stress and no mitigation effort taken
- Inadequate or disproportionate compensation
- Unions that may polarize workers from administration
- Weak problem-solving skills throughout the organization
- Lack of proper training and skills for high quality productivity
- Minimal ownership and participation at all levels of employee
- Failure to address stress, adversity and trauma with formal mitigation programs
- Reliance on rules to build productivity absent motivation and willing buy-in

The use of discipline, policy, cajoling, threat or other intimidation tactic is often applied to shake someone from lethargy to productivity. That may work, but generally it is for a short period of time and does not achieve sustainable change. And, often the individual, who is the focus of this attention, becomes more cautious and calculating to avoid getting caught. The single focus on the individual, without identifying their role within the larger organization, does not generally result in sustainable change. Lost is the rationale why the organization hired the person to perform specific job duties and when not fulfilled appropriately corrective action was necessary.

Screening, hiring and training someone to perform specific duties is expensive and time demanding. Seldom is the new employee asked to examine the organization's mission, vision, values, goals and objectives and to determine how they, as an employee, fit within that structure. These deficits diminish the performance of the new employee from day one on the job, how could it not? Discussion about their role and that of others within the mission et al., must take place in the orientation process, establishing the organization's expectations.

<u>Leader Assertion Guidelines.</u>

Clarity about role and performance can be among the more powerful of motivation strategies, if they are seen as practical and accomplish desired outcomes. Claims that the adoption of specific traits and characteristics will provide the tools for success, stretches the validity of actual achievement potential. Rather, we believe that there are certain truths or principles that can be adapted to a person's skills, knowledge, abilities and experience that provide an integrated approach to leadership. Traits and characteristics, grounded in focused applications, will enable others to align themselves into a more cohesive workforce. We call these truths assertions as their practiced application leads to confirmation of anticipated and expected outcomes.

Each of the leader assertions will be discussed with a description, highlights and example. The goal is not to provide "must follow" information, rather to allow the reader to assimilate relevant points and examples into their personal approach to employee oversight.

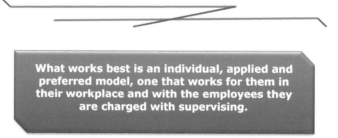

What works best is an individual, applied and preferred model, one that works for them in their workplace and with the employees they are charged with supervising.

As each assertion illustrates a separate approach or to establish a mindset that guides engagement and action, they are separate from the others. They do share aspects that serve to reinforce understanding and application. It is not my intent to say that learning and utilizing all twenty-five assertions is the key to excellent leadership, it is not. Repetition is present, for there are some actions, behaviors, and ways of thinking that are applicable to many situations. Bear with them, see how they apply to your needs and use them in positive ways.

Leadership is generally 95 percent doing what one does every day and 5 percent requiring a different approach to a solution or to move people in a different direction. It is within the five percent window we recommend seeing which assumptions might fit and review. One never knows how it will impact on the outcome!

Author

Richard C. Lumb, PhD, Lumb received his doctorate from Florida State University, and his Master and Bachelor degrees from the University of Southern Maine.

Lumb's academic career includes Chair and Program Director of Criminal Justice and Police Certification Training at Western Piedmont Community College, in Morganton, North Carolina. He was an Associate Professor, Department of Criminal Justice at the University of North Carolina at Charlotte; Associate Professor and Graduate Coordinator, Department of Criminal Justice at Northern Michigan University; and Chair and Associate Professor, Department of Criminal Justice, State University of New York at Brockport. He is Emeritus Associate Professor and Chair from SUNY Brockport. As an Associate Professor in the Department of Criminal Justice at the University of North Carolina at Charlotte, he was also the Director of the Research, Planning and Analysis Bureau at the Charlotte-Mecklenburg Police Department, under an agreement between the University and the City of Charlotte.

Lumb has over twenty-five years of direct police service and forty-years in the criminal justice, police and public safety system. He served with the Maine State Police, Chief of Police in Old Orchard Beach Maine, and as Chief of Police and Fire at the Morganton Department of Public Safety in Morganton, North Carolina. While completing his doctorate at Florida State University, Lumb worked for the Tallahassee Police Department, Tallahassee, Florida as Director of the E-911 Center and Community Officer Program.

Acknowledgments

<u>A Progression of Influences</u>

Many people have influenced the material in this manuscript. It began with a jolt of reality, when at seventeen years of age and just out of high school, I reported to Maine Maritime Academy as a first year Midshipman. Discipline and attention to detail swooped from the yardarm and made their presence directly felt. Failure of compliance to rules, dress code, improper response to an inquiry by an upper classman, and other infractions led to some form of reinforcement where a second chance was not an option. Graduation from high school did not prepare a person to switch from "milling with the crowd" to self-contained managing oneself and adherence to the rules and tradition. But, adaptation quickly occurs when demands require immediate response.

My first serious introduction to discipline, leadership, and compliance to expectations, came from upper-class Officer Rates (ranking officers). Charles E. Briggs was a midshipman Officer. Just out of high school and standing on the Quarterdeck of the S.S. State of Maine, Maine Maritime Academy's ship at the time, one quickly learns when, how, and why to respond in an expected and appropriate manner. As an Officer, his duty was to shake loose the boy and begin the journey to becoming a responsible adult. Sir Charles, you started me off right and kept tension on the line that continued all these years in many ways. I salute you with true respect across these many years from 1959 to today. Your continued friendship adds value to my life.

My years in the Maine State Police introduced me to many individuals whose leadership was inspirational. I met several excellent leaders in policing as I traveled that road for a number of years. Chief Dennis Nowicki, Charlotte-Mecklenburg Police Department will forever standout as he brought out the best in people, led them forward to new heights and demonstrated that life without change was wasting talent. At Charlotte-Mecklenburg Police Department, there were many who helped our Bureau to success due to their skills, abilities and commitment. They include: Dr. Elizabeth Groff, now faculty at Temple University; Monica Nguyen, Steve Eudy, and John Couchell at Charlotte-Mecklenburg; Amanda Neese, now Research Director at Gastonia Police Department, NC; Deputy Chief Stan Cook (Ret), CMPD; Captain and now Chief Terry Sult in Hampton, Va., and Harold Medlock, now Chief at Fayetteville Police Department in North Carolina; and others.

I worked with many fine officers who, in their way and style, led others forward, helped pick them up when they stumbled, and from those observations I questioned how well I stacked up to their example. They include Lieutenant Tim Deluca, Old Orchard Beach Police Department. And, the Morganton Department of Public Safety, then Lt. Johnny Wehunt, and who later was a Chief of Police in two communities.

A special word is needed. I met Ken Miller at Charlotte-Mecklenburg Police Department when I assumed Director of a new and merged research and planning Bureau. I had the good fortune of seeing him rise through the ranks, becoming Deputy Chief, having taken responsibility for several high profile projects. His careful analysis of issues, projects and challenges, coupled with innovation and a tenacity of getting the job done the right way, is appreciated and respected. He then served as Chief of Police of the Greensboro, North Carolina Police Department making many uplifting changes of benefit to the police and importantly with the community. As I write this, Chief Miller, begins his new job as Chief of Police in Greenville, South Carolina Police Department. His value of a police and community partnership to determine ways to improve the quality of life for all will inspire his officers and the citizens. I look forward to seeing those changes take place.

Chief Dana Kelley of the Old Orchard Beach Police Department, Maine came up through the ranks and has a long an honorable tenure in that community. He is a community advocate, his department works with citizens and others to improve the quality of life for everyone. He is respected for his management of police in a community whose proximity to the Atlantic Ocean sees tens of thousands of people descend for sun and surf every summer. He has taught me valuable lessons too, observing how he engages with his officers and citizens. Too often there are divisions that hamper community improvement. Not so in this example. He is a valued friend and colleague.

My second career focused on teaching at the university level and that too brought challenge. Influence, collaboration and friendship include Dr. Carol West, Dr. Charlie Dean, Dr. David Hirschel and others. My heart holds you close. And to my SUNY Brockport colleague, Professor Gary Metz, you bring joy to your students, progress to your work in important areas, and your long tenure as a police officer and Sheriff's Deputy. Your positive nature make people smile, a rare gift in today's world. I value your long friendship.

As a child of World War II, family taught me many things of value that suddenly pop into mind when a decision is being contemplated or when some action is emerging where a course of action has many intersections to navigate. So it seems we learn to walk, fall and get back up, with guiding hands reaching out to help a constant presence. To all, I remember and value what you so freely offered. Each family member has special leadership traits in the many things they do with others. Mostly self-taught, but with compassion for others, those present and those now gone give me daily images that bring a smile, a wonderment, and comfort to be part of it in this life.

This book is dedicated to my children, William, Pamela, Catherine and Melissa. In our collective existence all is possible and each one brings special talent, gifts, and special personality characteristics to the world.

And most important, supporting and helping an oft times capricious husband that demands patience, is a gift that my wife Paula offers in abundance. Without her support, all things are not possible. She assisted in construction of this book, editing, review, inquiry about concepts and hours of time. The result is a better read.

1. Leaders place the organization first and personal interest second.

It sometimes is difficult to remember that we are hired to do specific tasks or job functions and to obligate ourselves to those roles while employed. It is not uncommon that with time interests and the emergence of personal attention creeps in and we find some deviation taking place. We have experienced job boredom and in those situations we think broadly of what can be done to substitute a diversion. In policing, officers find some aspects of the job more fulfilling and exciting than others and when free time presents itself, they will engage in those duty functions, if not dissuaded by a supervisor.

There is room for experimentation, to seek newer ways of doing things, of applying new concepts or ideas to routine tasks with the intent of improvement or elevated motivation. However, arbitrary engagement in these endeavors, without seeking approval and support from the organization, may create unwanted opposition. Opportunity to improve certainly exists and when the organization adjusts and becomes a participating partner the chances of growth are greater than if going it alone. Seeking collaborative partnerships is the right choice of action for these reasons:

> ➤ We work for the organization and its continued existence is paramount.

> ➤ When we put ourselves first, the overall mission of the organization suffers.

> ➤ Leadership must consider mission and how it is fulfilled as first priority.

> ➤ Leaders can blend mission with individual skills and abilities as well as interests.

> ➤ The organization is the first priority.

It is also important to maximize employee time spend in fulfilling the organization's mission, vision, values and goals. If adherence to these four items are kept at the forefront of one's efforts, success is substantially more apt to occur than not. Supervisors, in collaboration with employees, need to address existing problems with the specific goal of sustainable solutions. Employee time spent in personal interest aspects may well moderate focus from duties the organization deems more important.

Innovation in schedule, planning, implementation and evaluation of outcomes is a powerful time saver, increases effectiveness and efficiency, and realigns everyone to mission. Blind delivery of services without examination of process, resource utilization and outcomes can be costly and inefficient.

<u>How the Employee Fits Within the Organization</u>

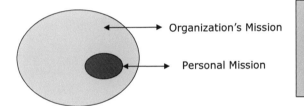

Organization's Mission

Personal Mission

It is less about self and more the employee's obligation to the organization and his or her job responsibilities.

Going to work for the pleasure it brings as a career choice and to be a loyal organization employee, ranges across several iterations. The continuum extends from no love of the job and strict focus on the individual to one where the organization is paramount. When you work only for your personal interests and needs, the organization and its purpose suffer in a negative way. The end result of why employees were hired and are employed is often ignored and left out of consideration. The differences may become oblivious.

Figure 1
Employee Allegiance Continuum

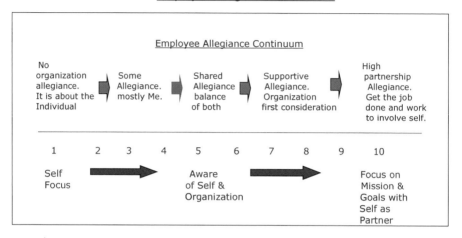

Example:

Discussions over contract demands and the refusal by the employer to agree or reject a counter offer to some work aspect, abounds. The outcome is gridlock, stalemate, anger, loss of productivity, motivation tanks, and disruption occurs.

So much has previously been granted that precious little remains for negotiation without losing control and direction. Mission and goals are seldom or never part of that conversation nor are the expected outcomes of both organization and employee. It should not be a one-way street and reasonable accommodation and innovation can often offer excellent results. And, depending on the product produced is there equal concern for client or customer. When challenged with "what about the citizen or clients?" that question often goes unanswered, resulting in blank stares and a huffy response. That mentality cannot exist or we lose effectiveness and efficiency and the overall purpose

Teamwork and collaboration are important if mission, vision, values, and goals are to be met effectively and efficiently

16

or organizational existence suffers. It can be no other way.

<u>What Can Be Done</u>

1. Discussions must occur about the roles and duties of employees within the organization. This includes expectations, performance, extent to which an open communications system exists, frequency of work related discussions, how problems are submitted and solutions obtained, types of communication venues, feedback and the performance evaluation system.

2. Leadership is not about position or rank; it reflects closer attunement to responsibility and effort. If you dwell on your rank or role and depend on that to carry the day, you will not be successful. While most people know who you are, it is often more about what you represent that is important.

3. Get out of your office and be among employees and the clients. A wall, door and possible window all work to contain you and provide isolation from where the rubber hits the road. I like to think a new office chair will last indefinitely as it will be seldom used. You cannot manage or lead others when you are not present or fully engaged with them.

4. Learn the mission and goals of the organization and contemplate what they mean to you and every one of the employees you supervise. If you cannot discuss them with specific meaning to each employee, how can they meet expectations? You are the ambassador of the organization to those you supervise, live the role in all its fullness.

Write your personal example.

Contemplating an example from your experience puts concepts   into perspective and allows you to mentally review what worked and what might have not been as successful. This is called "grounding" in your personal knowledge and experience, while also strengthening your overall value.

Questions to consider.

1. What differences exist between your example and experience and the organization's practices?

2. What was gained or lost in divergence from mission requirements?

3. What could be done to reconcile needs of organization and that of the employee that would bring benefit and advantage?

4. In hindsight, what might you have done differently?

---

2. Leaders are able to leverage employee and organizational outcomes versus the more common hierarchal and bureaucratic model.

Thinking in a circular manner, seeing up and down as well as side to side increases perspective and awareness. A narrow interpretation of policy, without a wider picture that examines the situation and conditions of all potential interested parties, limits perspective. It is also critical that attention on employees is kept at the forefront of thinking and attention. An outward focus may ignore the organization's employees, who at the center of service delivery, are of primary value. The following statements relate to organizations and people and pertain to supervisor awareness.

> ➤ If we only think vertically, we lose the horizontal perspective and vice versa.

> ➤ Leaders must know their employees and seek to match their motivation and interests with the organization.

> ➤ Focus must be on the end result, customer or service outcome. When consideration shifts to the employee only preference, loss occurs.

> ➤ Leaders must be cognizant that people and mission may conflict and find ways to bridge division of purpose.

> ➤ Having a frank and informative discussion with employees to assure they are familiar with the organization's mission, vision, values and goals and to discuss how they fit with the employees' knowledge, skills and experience is an absolute critical supervisor role.

> ➤ We cannot assume the employee knows and understands. Where would they acquire that knowledge unless someone spent time with them in discussion? This also holds true for employees with five, ten and more years of service. Change evolves and employees must keep pace.

> ➤ Review and realignment is critical as bad habits, culture change and other influences intercede with individual attitudes skewing the alignment between employees and the organization they work for. A one-on-one meeting and discussion will head off future issues that can be destructive to all parties. Drift is a natural fact of employment for we are subject to colleagues, experience and other influences that may take us further away from the core mission and purpose of working for an organization.

Bureaucratic Model[2]   **Networks & Innovation Model**[3]

Example:

Insuring that the employee is familiar with expectations, fit within the organization, and the roles of supervisors often fills a critical gap.

Captain Stan Cook, a District Commander[4] at the Charlotte-Mecklenburg Police Department in North Carolina, initiated an excellent model for the indoctrination of new officer recruits into the field. His normal practice was to take a newly graduated police academy recruit and have the first meeting when that officer reported for duty. Captain Cook had the new officer's Sergeant present as well. The purpose was to discuss expectations, policy, and how the district operated within the larger police department. It was a simple and brilliant approach to officer orientation. The department's and District's expectations were conveyed regarding the delivery of service within the community problem oriented policing model, officer performance, and performance evaluation were discussed. The officer was asked about his or her expectations, goals and why they had chosen to be a police officer. Other issues that had previously caused problems were put on the table and discussed so the new officer would understand why actions did or did not occur. When the meeting ended, the new officer was very aware

---

[2] en.wikipedia.org359 × 366
[3] http://www.dreamstime.com
[4] Later a Deputy Chief of Police

20

of what was expected; parameters on behavior and performance, and all of his or her questions were answered.

It is appropriate to say that this District was generally first among police districts in citizen and officer satisfaction. Part of the reason for this was the commander's orientation and the time and effort explaining the department's mission and other accompanying values.

Policy, rule and procedures are also of value. Discussion and explanation must occur as we can never assume that the employee understands and is able to apply them to work situations. They are important in working with employees, helping them to perform their duties appropriately, drawing upon their motivation and interests, and creating a partnership that results in mutual benefit.

What Can Be Done

1. We frequently focus on the present moment to such an extent we lose peripheral sight. Left to its own stasis (state of no change) and without supervisor awareness or intervention, a level of performance may emerge that represents complacency, personal comfort and disconnect from the organization itself.

2. Only an engaged supervisor and leader can make a difference in performance and output. At each level of an organization, we tend to perform our tasks and responsibilities in as constant manner, but often with personal bias and preference. Mostly natural behavior in and of itself, but, this is not sufficient if you are a leader and supervisor of others, as you have a larger role to play.

3. Motivation and remaining on task, excellent performance in an effective and efficient manner are all examples of terms that abound regarding an organization and its employees. Lofty to be sure, but still just terms unless they are operationalized by supervisors with their employees and carefully integrate the organization's mission and goals in performance.

4. While it is more work than simply adhering to orders, compliance with policy and a single focus on the bottom-line, engaging with employees as often as needed builds personal expectation and clarity. Employees are different in outlook, motivation and performance and job descriptions aside, disparities exist and can be maximized to achieve goals. You must know each person who reports to you. While work rules are prohibitive at times, you cannot achieve collaboration by being stiff, by the book, remote and aloof to other people. If this attitude is present, supervisory achievement will suffer.

5. Discussion and conversation about work, training needs, equipment, goals and all other matters that may present themselves are foundational to working with others in maximizing performance. Put rank or power of position on the shelf, it is not going anywhere, and truly engages with people. Responsibility and collaboration is a two-way street that you and the employees utilize on a daily basis.

Write your personal example.

```



```

Questions to Consider.

1. How familiar are you with the philosophy and expectations of your boss and his or her boss as well?

2. Can you explain to your supervisees why certain procedures and actions are taken within the larger concept of the organization?

3. Are you able to present a vision for the performance of employees in your section to allow them a broader understanding of their role?

4. Do you and your supervisees discuss motivation, what inhibits it, what can be done to improve, and how to maintain a positive work environment?

3. Leaders continually perfect their role and responsibilities.

Stagnation is a serial killer in many organizations. Your supervisor job description provides general parameters and outline of the duties and role you carry. Seldom are the details of supervisory performance duties and expectations sufficient. Unfortunately, it is the individual who will face the risk of becoming ineffective or automated in that role. There is no substitute for staying on top of the game and current with best practices, separating what is important from the mundane, and being aware of your people and their needs and aspirations. You should make sure, before they even walk in the door, that future error will be minimalized. Mastering this requires diligent work, keeping a record or what works and what does not, along with experimentation and feedback to name a few. Some ideas that help toward perfecting your role and responsibilities are as follows:

➤ Being responsible to the organization and employees represents two of a three-part triune. The first and most critical part involves taking an inventory of people, resources, role and other job indicators. While we may acknowledge professional (and personal) drift occurring in our employees or other colleagues, it also happens to us. Change occurs and we may not always be aware. This lack of self-awareness of personal drift diminishes our effectiveness.

➤ Ask for feedback, it is not a secret ballot that results in ridiculous and ineffective gibberish, but utilizes a planned and well thought out survey. For example: Plan a meeting with one or two representatives from among those who report to you. Assign them the task, as representatives, to talk with peers within your supervisee group to bring in constructive responses before the meeting occurs where the survey will be discussed. A representative attending an exchange meeting, whose purpose is to seek improvement, is a positive way to remain connected to the larger group. It allows employees to communicate their ideas or concerns. It is important to not let this feedback meeting disintegrate into a "bitch session," as that accomplishes little. It is a good idea to set the meeting guidelines and expectations before the meeting begins.

➤ Ask yourself: What have you seen in others that you felt were excellent leadership skills? What were the things they said, did or encouraged you to do that was impressive? We generally work with and for a number of people in our careers and there are a few who stand out in our thinking as individuals who were trustworthy, who gave their all, and made others feel important to the organization. These same individuals were able to motivate, help and assist, to encourage and to stand with those in need of a strong arm or who were willing to listen. These are important people with important character traits, as they bring lessons and illustrations that you can use in your current position. Spend some time considering them and what they meant to you, and in turn, use those tactics in your working relationships.

➤ You cannot be all things to all people, nor is it feasible to expect that you should or must be. Each and every encounter, within your role as supervisor and your position as an employee for the larger organization, demands a different skill, knowledge or ability set that is applicable to each situation and moment that arises. When you encounter this level of diversity, your experience kicks in and you intuitively know what needs to be done. If you listen to yourself within the moment, and consider the options you can take, you will make thoughtful and informed choices. This allows you to emerge as a thoughtful and helpful leader who is able to make sound decisions that lead to appropriate outcomes.

Figure 3.1

Influences on Decisions

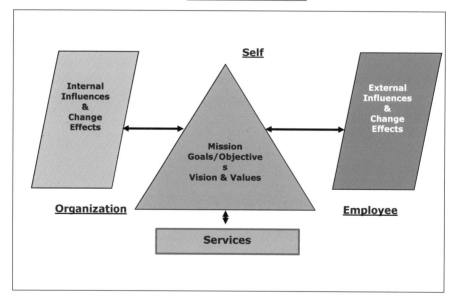

Example:

As a Sergeant, Robert mapped out what he learned from others who had been promoted, and the important and critical steps leading to their promotions. He made a list of the colleges they attended and associated them with career points. He determined that he needed to complete a master's degree and chose a college program that focused on a business and administrative track. He applied for and soon enrolled in the program of study of his choice. Over an extend period, Robert completed the degree that he hoped would take him the next step toward promotion.

Robert immediately sought within his organization a variety of experiences and assignments that would expanding his skills and knowledge across the organization. He engaged with personnel under his direction and worked to improve their performance and value to the organization. He worked with the community, neighborhoods, and other city departments to address issues and problems associated with matters of importance and value. He methodically asked others for input into his performance. All of these steps resulted in steady and consistent rise through the ranks to the number two position (Deputy Chief) in a large police department of over 2000 employees.

➢ A prime responsibility of the organization is to keep its leadership team at the top of their game. This means investing time and money into leadership and encouraging continuing education as a means of allowing growth and fostering professional motivation within the organization.

➢ The skills, knowledge, abilities, attitude and experience of a person, in a leadership role, must be determined and a plan for their continued application and growth devised. Sometimes this may occur from a personal, external track of education and training, but oftentimes it can and should be provided as an internal opportunity for training and development, within the organization, geared to the requisite skills and expected knowledge and abilities.

What Can Be Done

1. When you think you know your job, stop and take inventory. What are you addressing well, what is mediocre and what needs to change? The inventory presents you with a goal chart that can be used to map out steps needed to improve and increase knowledge and its applicability to the organization, its mission and goals, for both yourself and the employees you supervise.

The chart below is to assist in considering a related course of action.

Chart 3.1
Personal Tools

Skill, Knowledge, Ability & Experience Necessary to my job performance	1. **Insufficient** SKAE's and needed at this time.	2. **Moderate** SKAE's and improvement is deemed helpful.	3. **Satisfactory** SKAE's to perform duties.	4. **Advanced** SKAE's available, being used, and available to help others.
❖				
List and describe your current status under appropriate columns.	Identify components for this rated area.	Identify components for this rated area.	Identify components for this rated area.	Identify components for this rated area.
1.				
Areas where improvement or sharing of your personal skills can assist others.	Check list of steps to address for improvement.	Check list of steps to address for improvement.	Check list of steps to address for increased SKAE.	How can you help others acquire for themselves?
	a.	a.	a.	a.
	b.	b.	b.	b.
	c.	c.	c.	c.
	d.	d.	d.	d.
2.				
Areas where improvement or sharing of your personal skills can assist others.	Check list of steps to address for improvement.	Check list of steps to address for improvement.	Check list of steps to address for increased SKAE.	How can you help others acquire for themselves?
	a.	a.	a.	a.
	b.	b.	b.	b.
	c.	c.	c.	c

❖

2. Continue filling in the chart for additional SKAE's you wish to address. This need not be an exhaustive list and it should not commandeer your work life. This is meant to help identify where strengths and weaknesses may lie

and what you recommend for a self-improvement plan. This is also a useful experience for your employees when addressing their goals and aspirations.

Write your personal example.

Questions to Consider.

1. Are you able to clearly articulate your role and duties within the organization?

2. Are there examples of personal drift from the organization's mission, vision, values and goals? If so, do you need to address realignment?

3. What makes you a thoughtful person? Are these traits helpful to others and if so, in what ways?

4. Leaders leverage resources and relationships to achieve success.

Leveraging is not about blame, right-sizing, down-sizing or ostracizing, it is about working within the system and pulling together resources and people to be successful in what you, and those who report to you, are expected to achieve. Start with those closest to the need or issue and branch out as you become clear on what is expected and what must be done to overcome barriers to successful change. A match generally does not ignite and illuminate if kept closed in a box. It must be removed, provided with tension on a source that will produce the change from sulfur and an oxidizing agent to flame. The same with people, when we open the world of possibility to the light that emerges, it will frequently guide the desired change.

> ➢ Work is not always a routine event. We often see repetitive effort where employees habitually perform their duties in the same manner. This is comfortable and provides for few disagreeable moments, conflict or change. The "just leave me alone to do my job" may be heard, but what we are not hearing (yet seeing, if we look closely), is an unwillingness to do something different, provide an elevated amount of energy and effort, and a reluctance to step out of a long established comfort zone.

> ➢ Faced with a new task or problem to solve, supervisors are required to find solutions. They can order that something be done, which is appropriate when other alternatives are not a consideration. However, even orders from a supervisor become repetitive and mundane, and employees often respond with apathy and complacency. The goal is to overcome lethargy and increase motivation and effort into fulfilling the task at hand. Otherwise, this lack of action frequently fails to lead to sustainable outcomes, with the problem resurfacing again and again. The "just leave me alone" comment is replaced with "not my problem!"

> ➢ Resources include personnel, tools and equipment, programs, planning, solicitation and other actions that seek to fulfill the resolution to the original problem. Conduct an inventory, if necessary, to insure all resources are covered or available. When time allows, it is generally advisable for the leader to do the following:

> a) Assemble the group.

> b) Lay out the task or issue to be addressed, clearly, in detail, and answer all related questions.

c) Ask for input from those assembled. We are often positively surprised by the depth and strong contribution by members of a group, who, when asked have things worthwhile to offer.

d) Record the offered comments or suggested solutions under the task or problem so everyone can see what is developing.

e) Add in your own comments and knowledge of the parameters on what can be done.

f) Seek consensus on the best course of action and, if possible, implement it. Determine who will be involved, the extent of their involvement along with specific duties, and dismiss those that are no longer needed toward completion of the project.

g) Spend time in grounding everyone on the project team in what has to be done, how and who will do what aspects of the task. Deadlines and a timetable are helpful to allow milestones for progress. If an evaluation is to be done, also advise the group of its content. A "no surprises" approach is the right one to follow. Determine how information and progress will be tracked and recorded and who the "go to" person is for direction and task approval.

h) Bring relevant resources and people to the table to insure that sufficient personnel and support is in place and can be drawn on as needed. To send the team off without proper supervision, resources and other required support is not only a recipe for failure for the team, but is a failure in leadership.

i) Record outcomes and prepare for a post-incident review to learn from the process. Share outcomes with participants.

Chart 4.1
Leveraging Chart

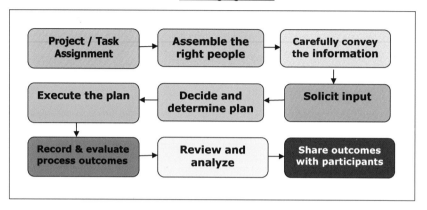

EXAMPLE:

The identification of an apartment where police were called frequently to quell noise and argument eventually led to asking the question, "What can be done to eliminate the problem?" Continued police response was not producing a sustainable solution and the likelihood of being called via 911 again was high. Analysis of the calls for service data to that apartment disclosed over 60 calls in one year. The cost and time of responding demanded a solution.

What Can Be Done (Example used can be applied to any organization)

1. Examination of the problem to learn of its component parts will lead to a more in-depth knowledge base of the people, place, frequency of calls, what was done and outcomes. Understanding what was done previously is also of critical information, for without this depth of knowledge, sustainable solutions are more elusive.

2. If prior intervention was not successful, it is unlikely that the same response will achieve different results. The question becomes, "what can be done? While procedures will follow the agencies policy, there are some check sheet steps that are important. They include:

> Conduct an in-depth discussion of potential solutions within the context of the identified problem.
> Who else should be included in the examination?

30

> What does analysis of the data gathered on this particular issue say?
> What are probable solutions to bringing resolution to the problem?
> Develop a plan and insure that it is comprehensive addressing the issue and all that data gathering and analysis offers as information.

Seeking a solution based on full knowledge of the facts and parallel information helps to clarify the issue. Calling on another agency for assistance strengthens collaboration, breadth of solution, deeper examination of sustainable solutions, and a pathway to resolution.

Write your personal example.

Questions to consider.

1. Do you occasionally conduct an inventory of your employees to determine needs, gripes, and suggestions and to identify areas for change consideration? What is it you do?

2. Do you clearly explain new tasks and solicit input and feedback from employees?

3. What methods do you use to keep your staff informed?

4. When engaged in problem identification and then seeking sustainable solutions, what is the process you engage in to include stakeholders?

5. Leaders look beyond day-to-day activities and incorporate a future focus.

The effect of the mundane can be both security and boredom. When challenge diminishes, employees often seek to fill the void with other interests that may or may not represent the work they do. When it does not, productivity, commitment and attention to detail usually suffer. If a person wants to do crossword puzzles on their computer at home, fine, but at work, it is unacceptable!

Whether we realize it or not, we often encapsulate a person in one form of isolation or another, stifle communication, remove excitement and innovation and wonder why low performance is happening. Is there any wonder? We all have worked for a boss who adhered to the mantra of children, that you should be "seen and not heard!" And so our employees become robotic in nature, non-contributory, their motivation in the tank and innovation out the window! And, then we are surprised when performance drops.

Today's worker and work environment has many examples. Over time it becomes boring, lacks challenge, and demands nothing and eventually it is a chore to come to work.

> **Leaders engage employees in the events of the day, motivate their interest and ideas, and with others determine how positive change and growth can occur.**

The role of a leader is not to entertain or create events for the sake of having them. The real leader assumes responsibility for hiring self-motivated, easily engaged, cooperative and collaborative individuals who are able to work well in their position, to communicate their ideas and their needs with their supervisors. Supervisors help each individual maximize their value to the organization and to rise above their personal "comfort zone." A good leader will find ways to keep their employees' interest, commitment and creativity alive. The key to doing so involves the ability of the leader to openly and easily engage with each employee, to ask for input and ideas, and to provide them with opportunities for involvement and education.

Questions

1. What are you doing today that can be improved upon for tomorrow?

2. Can you help the employee learn new skills and knowledge for their personal growth?

3. Are you aware of and on top of the latest motivational techniques for the jobs you supervise?

4. Do you allow in-put and hold discussions with members of your group; explore possibilities and potential with others?

5. Are you an advocate for "your people" and provide for them when possible while still considering the mission and goals of the organization?

6. Are you staying abreast of changes and influences to the jobs, services and products of the organization and how they impact on your employees?

EXAMPLE:

When the City of Charlotte and the Charlotte-Mecklenburg Police Department made the decision to adopt community problem oriented policing to replace a more traditional crime control model, successful achievement would include the community and neighborhood residents. There could be no division. The sought after outcome was the establishment of a partnership, collaboration with mutual effort toward an agenda of change.

The City's Neighborhood Development Department formed collaboration with the Police Department to bring citizens to the table. This process included training, moderating meetings, identifying neighborhood leadership and helping them to be successful.

In this new venue police had to change their communication style with citizens, be open to listening, to working collaboratively and being advocates of and to the community. The goal was the identification of long-standing problems and using a model that was developed by Herman Goldstein whose focus was achieving sustainable solutions. To do this, it was not business as usual. It involved continuous review, data collection and evaluation, meeting with citizens and working through many questions, identifying barriers and selecting a best possible path to a viable solution. The new goal was to improve the quality of life of communities, one that forced a long-term view, not just addressing day-to-day needs.

What Can Be Done

1. Get your house in order.
2. Keep lists and keep them updated.
3. Engage in conversation with people.
4. Hold occasional group conversations.
5. Plan, project and track progress toward goals.

1. Get your house in order. Be able to break-down tasks and work focus into short and long-term plans. The tendency is to work on the issue at the moment under the belief "the future will take care of itself." Foolish thinking, at best!

2. Keep lists and keep them updated. It does not have to be formal or use sophisticated technology. Their purpose is for recall. If you start one, refer to it frequently and update regularly. It is worth the time and assists in your organization and that of employees.

3. Engage in conversation with a broad range of individuals involved in the identified process or goal. Pass along information and be willing and open to receiving it. We put too much stock in formal systems, which in turn are often ignored and prove to be of little value.

4. Hold occasional group conversations to tell each other where things stand, what the goal continues to be, the barriers being encountered and to hear from one another. Information void is a major inhibitor to change and acquisition of positive outcomes.

5. Plan, project and track progress toward goals. You must engage with the future and anticipate what might be encountered, or it will take you by surprise when least expected. Plans change and alter as new information arrives: remain open and flexible in the planning and direction you take to reach your desired goal/outcome. Unless you take a future focus on some of the responsibilities you carry, you cannot be as effective as hoped.

Write your example.

Questions to consider.

1. What tactics do you use to keep your employees on task?

2. When you observe straying from assigned tasks, how to you handle that personnel situation?

3. Do you use different methods to address older or longer term employees than those who were hired within the past five to ten years?

6. Leaders manage immediate and short-term needs while anticipating change, growth and future direction.

Daily demands range from a "put it off until tomorrow" or the opposite, "to saddle up and get going" as this is serious stuff. The best of plans are often interrupted with unexpected requests or crises that appear without warning. Disruption of plans can be unsettling and when routine requires change, people react in multiple ways.

We are often complacent due to the comfort of routine and habit, not having to anticipate that something may occur and require adaptation. People become protective of the status quo and will often resist, sometimes strenuously, maintaining the comfort that accompanies knowing what to expect.

Each morning, we begin the day following a fairly consistent routine. That same set of personal rules follows you to work. It is comfortable and expected. If you doubt that you are a creature of habit, put your watch on the opposite arm tomorrow and wear it that way throughout the day. It will drive you nuts!

We relate to change depending on the extent to which it impacts on us and those around us, and within our mental perspective of what and how things should be. Most of us do not like the day that was planned in one fashion only to be changed or altered. It is frustrating and unsettling, much of the time.

When alert to the environment, news and information and looking ahead to anticipate what might be encountered, plans can be devised, kept in reserve and referred to if the occasion were to present itself.

Routine is both a blessing and a hindrance when we consider the needs of the organization and the employees. However, the question of what to do about it is complex and highly dependent on organizational policy, culture, and habit. But, no leader should sit still and worry about change efforts, for not to do so is to become stagnant.

When change is eminent, that announcement does not generally result in willing compliance, especially, when resistance is allowed by complacent supervisors and administrators. Announcement of the intended change is the first step in a process that allows employees the opportunity to seek answers, to weigh consequences and benefits, and hopefully adapt to new ways of conducting both personal and organizational business. Without clear explanation and discussion, many employees simply shrug off new ideas and seek to maintain current behaviors. They will not be able to maintain a "no-change" attitude for all times, as the organization will move forward, making it important to address issues before they occur.

When change is proposed, fully 40 percent of employees will be in what Prochaska labels Precontemplation, thinking about change but staying close to what they currently do until more information is available to raise their comfort level. Another 40 percent will contemplate change, making minor adjustment but continue to observe before any substantive change takes place. Tem percent will begin to make changes, the preparation stage, and the final 10 percent will take action and embrace change moving directly into it. This is not to say that these groupings are cast in cement for they are not, they give general attitude and behavior actions by employees. The important point is, by talking, explaining and receiving input from employees, we are able to lessen the challenges of bringing about change in an organization. Giving a direct order, may not be as effective as we once thought.

Prochaska's Readiness to Change Model[5]

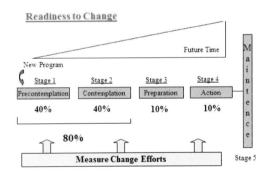

Managers must be willing to listen as well as talk for effective communications to take place. When employees are allowed to discuss their needs and issues, managers must be prepared to deal with what they hear (O'Neill, 1999[6]). The common modern day memo by e-mail may be one of

---

[5] Prochaska, J., & DiClemente, C. (1982). Transtheoretical therapy: Toward a more integrative model of change. Psychotherapy: Theory, Research and Practice. 276-288.
[6] O'Neill, M (1999). Communicating for change. CMS Management, June, 73, 22-25.

the worst inventions for organizations know presently. Lost is the face-to-face discussion, the opportunity to ask questions, to offer input and to explore alternatives. People, when relegated to obscurity, will follow their own path, to the extent possible.

It is critically important for managers to provide clear rationale for change and to assist employees in being successful in carrying out their evolving job responsibilities. Underlying issues of change is the fear of failure, whenever someone is coerced to do something differently, where success and pitfalls are not known or understood by the individual (Shimon, 2011[7]).

EXAMPLE:

Anticipating several early retirements due to a change in how the city funded employee health benefits, the Chief of Police pondered the fact that six of his eleven administrative staff can retire and the majority are saying they will, if the City Council changes the health insurance policy.

It is a good time for three of the six to retire as they have become less effective over the years and show signs of lethargy and loss of motivation. They can be replaced with the proper promotional process. The remaining three administrators are serving critical roles in the department and planning is necessary for their replacement.

The Chief considers the overall implications and attempts to put priorities to the pending decisions and action steps.

What Can Be Done

1. Short term gap filling is the first priority once it is known what the six administrators are going to do. Preliminary planning can take place on who will best fit the need. Having a preliminary discussion with potential replacements may or may not be possible depending on contractual agreements and policy.

2. Call a meeting with all staff who indicated they may retire to ascertain new information and to set the stage for decision-making. Advise what your intended steps might be as sharing information will help with ease of action when the time comes.

---

[7] Shimon, U. (2011). Fear and Anxiety: effective managerial tools or harmful and jeopardizing factors? *Far East Journal of Psychology & Business*; Nov. 5(2), 1-12.

3. Determine what steps are necessary to fill positions in a temporary capacity. What are the department, city or town policy? Obtain input and help from the human resource person most able to assist.

4. Clear future actions with the city or town manager to pave the process eliminating speed bumps or barriers that can be addressed early.

5. As change is anticipated, determine if additional changes would be beneficial during this period and if so begin that planning. Taking advantage of a change opportunity reduces the unexpected action that is occasionally necessary.

6. Review best practices that are taking place and determine if any of them would be appropriate for your agency. If they are deemed of value, assemble a group to discuss them and seek input before making a decision to proceed. Removing as many rumor opportunities and obtaining input from a broad swath of the department reduces future complaint and resistance.

7. Make plans, write them down, establish time-lines and chart progress with any of the changes that become necessary.

Write your example.

Questions to consider.

1. How do you minimize distractions from duty assignments?

2. Do you allow employees, when time and resources allow, taking on some personal venture, within the job parameters that they have an interest in?

3. Do you have routine meetings with you staff to discuss changes, ideas and innovations? What are the general outcomes of these meetings, if held?

7. Leaders continually scan internal and external environments, adjust plans, manage resources, and direct employees to fulfill the mission efficiently and effectively.

Going about daily business, in a routine and habitual manner, works when all is in balance and harmony. When the going is rough and different pressure points are being experienced, emotional reaction is the norm and it does not always produce desired outcomes. It is during these times that supervisors and leadership must be its most innovative and effective. Waiting it out may well result in worsening conditions.

One's office can be inhibiting, provide a barrier to open exchange, and a place away from the fray and therefore safe from demands. A door is indicative that the individual is protected from the day to day business activities that are in play.

Available and engaged is a preferred business style and one that generally serves you well,

Leaders often become bogged down in paper work. Being office bound inhibits knowing what is taking place with employees, work demands, satisfaction issues and a host of other markers that reflect operational harmony. The desk and office equipped with telephone, computer, internet and departmental systems is a huge draw as the need to remain in communication pulls strongly on us all. But, it can be argued that remaining isolated is in itself a giant inhibitor knowing what is happening.

When we think about what is important it is often helpful to make a list of those items or equipment/electronics. Then rank order the list from most important to least important, adding facts or other pertinent information as you go along. Then determine what items on the list actually need to be in your office. Perhaps you will find that many of those items are based upon want vs. need, or are subjected to not being connected to your office at all. Be honest with yourself, your organization, your position and your mission statement with decision-making. This will help you get a clear picture about exactly what you need to have in your office, including yourself, after all.

When office walls define your boundaries, you are effectively "out of the loop," regardless of the beliefs you have that it is not so. The work is being done external to your office and probably outside the building. Staying within the protection of those safe walls does not allow you to be an effective, informed or connected leader.

The action lies where personnel deliver services and engage with customers. To know what is taking place you need to enable yourself to see, smell, hear, touch and engage in aspects of that world. The totality of experience cannot be replicated anecdotally or after an event occurs, while sitting in the protective environment of an office.

Engaging with employees portrays a positive message of who you are as a leader. It allows your employees/supervisees the opportunity to connect with you in a more personal way. It opens the lines of communication and creates a feeling of caring and commitment to them and to the organization. If you engage with your employees on a regular basis, acceptance of your presence is not an issue and you will feel the benefit from your own engagement and participation.

While out in the field and at work sites, ask questions, examine procedures, and look at what takes employee time with the duties they perform. Compare what is being done with expectations and match them to the overall mission and goals of the organization. Is everything compatible and are employees working for the organization in the best ways possible? If not, you and employees must engage in a discussion on how corrections will take place.

If change is needed, solutions can be found. Unless an emergency arises, always obtain input to your own comments and feedback about what is being observed and what needs changing. Some of the most productive feedback and suggestions for change will come from your direct line staff, the people who are in the field doing difficult jobs. It is a wise leader who is not afraid to surround him or her with strong workers. This connection begins and strengthens by creating opportunities for dialogue and feedback. Do not isolate yourself from employees, as it only creates suspicion, complaint and division. Inclusiveness is a powerful tool, as is the empowerment of your workers. Neither of these can be brought to fruition unless trust and familiarity exist.

Revise plans and operational focus as needed but do so openly and with input. To do otherwise is to establish barriers that may be difficult to overcome.

EXAMPLE:

Sgt. Stephanie Howard was a supervisor over nine second shift police officers serving the Baker Section of a large city. The commanding Captain was a "paper work" advocate and insisted the Sergeants keep all reports current and their desk cleared.

Doing so required many hours in the office, processing paperwork and not knowing what was happening on the street except for the occasional radio calls overheard or those "after the event" discussions. The field officers realized that the Sergeant was required to spend long hours in the office and thus they (field officers) went about the work as they deemed appropriate. As long as the paper work was complete and submitted they were seldom "bothered" or observed.

Changes would take place in the community being patrolled, new issues arising from time to time, and citizen expectations being voiced as community concerns increased or decreased. Gradually, the second shift officers moved to a patrol model that fit individual interests. Many of these interests were not in compliance with the department's mission and goals, such as preferring to run radar, looking for drunk drivers, or spending time in non-police endeavors. The productivity greatly diminished, response to calls took longer and the level of citizen complaints increased.

The Captain summoned the Sergeant and ranted about the lack of supervision and the slipshod work being done. He did not ask the Sergeant her perspective, instead saying, "You need to get your people in line!"

Sgt. Howard left the Captain's office in a foul frame of mind, angry, unable to rationalize what his problem was, because he was, after all, the person who insisted on getting the paper work done in the first place. Rationalizing a path to correction is not possible in this moment, as all parties are angry and listening skills have most likely shut down. But, this condition could not sustain itself, change has to be made and soon.

What Can Be Done

1. Guard against complacency and comfort. Your office should not provide a cocoon, or protection from your responsibilities.

2. Pay attention to people working for you. Be part of their work world and engage in discussion with them on a regular basis.

3. Challenge routine and examine who is making an impact on the work being performed, to what extent, and the causes and outcome experienced because of them. A leader may be a barrier to external and some internal forces that interrupt work and create uncomfortable situations. When interruptions take place that are distracting, cause errors, and effectively reduce productivity, it is time to engage in finding solutions. An example is someone wandering by, stopping to talk with a friend who is hard at work at that time. Visiting others is not wrong, but timing and consideration of what is taking place at that time, is part of the mix.

4. If you have plans that guide work expectations, review them often and include those employees who are affected by the performance plan. Seek their input and observations regarding how the plan is working, or not. Change is inevitable and if it is prompted by self-initiated action, it is a far better choice than a sudden unexpected change in the rules, plan or routine.

5. Examine mission and goals and compare them to the work being done by your unit. Are the goals being met? Are the core mission statement and values being addressed and demonstrated by the performance of your workers and the outcome of their efforts? Are there bumps in the road that need to be addressed? If some incompatibility exists, determine what needs to be done to fix it. Then, fix it!

6. Keep your employees in the loop and include them in discussions and planning. When we assume we are the only player on the team, it will suffer. Motivation, inclusion and feelings of individual worth and higher levels of personal and professional investment emerge when a team approach is taken. Also, it is all too easy to blame someone else when you have not participated in the policy or procedures being questioned.

7. It is good practice to extend this "loop" of communication and team work by including your supervisor in discussions and planning on a consistent basis. Having an open ended conversation with your supervisor goes a long way in creating a transparent operations and will help in the typical "How come I didn't know/hear about this sooner" event from occurring when the occasional problem arises.

8. Ask your customer base what they think of the services received. Ask what is working really well and what isn't. Inquire of their ideas and observations. This will be informative and have a positive payoff for both the providers of service and the recipient. Knowing what is appreciated and well received allows for strengthening that which is going well. We often forget to ask those who received the service for their evaluation and comments. That type of missing information could well make the difference from highly satisfied to disgruntled.   When we overlook this critical group of consumers, we are missing a priceless opportunity to find out what needs to be fixed, or, even more importantly, to find out what it is that we are doing really well, so we can continue to do it!

Write your example.

Questions to consider.

1. Do you feel you are in the communications loop both organizationally and within your section or unit?

2. How often during a work week do you engage directly with employees at their place of work?

3. How do you deal with conflict?

4. How do you insure that your views and observations are incorporated in policy?

8. Leaders are visionary with regard to their organization's mission and purpose.

Unless a leader conveys a vision to his or her employees, they will draw on their own assumptions or perspectives. Leaders must formulate a vision of services, performance, mission and goals and then clearly convey it to employees. Communicating that vision is critical and requires definition and example so adequate grounding takes place. Add to this the necessity for discussion to occur at a formal meeting to allow asking questions, clarification provided and to determine how well reality coexists in the workplace.

Discuss what indicators will demonstrate success in achieving the vision and help individuals incorporate them into their behavior and personal philosophy. Differences must be resolved to insure that everyone is on the same page. Once comfort is realized with employee understanding, then measuring compliance to that vision must take place. Vision must be compatible with mission, for the organization comes first and foremost.

Brown, Yoshioka and Munoz (2004)[8] define mission in the following manner: *"Organizations rely on their mission to attract resources and guide decision-making. The mission is more than a statement or a symbol; it is a tool that provides a clear, compelling statement of purpose that is disseminated both internally and externally. Increasingly mission statements are recognized as a strong management tool that can motivate employees and keep them focused on the purpose of the organization"*.

Mission declares the purpose, path and promotion of what the organization does to provide service. Vision is a conceptual model of what the leader wants and expects from employee effort and performance, within the parameters of the mission. Goals and objectives emerge from the vision and they, in turn, provide benchmarks to measure compliance to them. This need not be a punitive effort; rather, it serves to allow individuals to measure their own progress and fit. A common sense of purpose, direction and expectation often guide motivation and action.

Vision is a goal to which employees can aspire, as it pulls the organization forward in meeting demands, fulfilling mission and achieving excellence. Both the internal and external environments are important. It is not a one or

[8] Brown, W., Yoshioka, C., & Munoz, P. (2004). Organizational Mission as a Core Dimension in Employee Retention. Journal of Park and Recreation Administration, 22(2), 28*43.

the other situation, for both must coincide and remain harmonious. Otherwise the mission and vision cannot be achieved with a high degree of success.

We often expect employees to know and understand the mission, vision, values and goals, but do not insure that is true. When the train leaves the track, it is often because of a flaw in the foundation of what makes things work. When that happens we are often shocked and befuddled. We need not be. Few organizations take the time to train and discuss these factors with employees. And, importantly, periodic review is also a critical component to insure compliance.

At the Charlotte-Mecklenburg, NC, Police Department, the vision was community problem oriented policing (CPOP), a change from the traditional approach that primarily used law enforcement as the tool for dealing with community issues and needs. The time was the mid-1990s, and a new Chief of Police was hired to redirect the agency forward in mission and vision as well as technological enhancements to guide decision-making, planning and program development.

The departments patrol, investigative and all other units had completed basic training in the new model and more extensive and specialized training was taking place. The Chief determined that he would attend each shift's "check on" and field questions about CPOP. Following a brief discussion of the progress being made, the Chief asked if there were any questions from the officers present. One officer raised his hand and, when acknowledged, simply said, *"This CPOP bullshit won't work!"* Okay, that was up front, for sure! The Chief asked the officer if he would consent to his riding with him for one shift so they might explore the concept. The officer's response was, *"How about tonight Chief?"*

That ride-along was accepted and the chief, in uniform, met with the officer and spent the shift with him. As calls were dispatched and the officer responded, the chief inquired if the officer had been to that location previously, was he familiar with the people who were the focus of the officer's attention, what had been done in the past to resolve issues, and other defining questions. With the replies made, scenarios were presented that posed what the officer might have done, and could do in the future to moderate or prevent future calls for service from that location. At the end of the shift, the officer was asked to select one major problem that he and the community agreed was problematic.

That problem was identified (example: multiple calls to the same family within a public housing unit in the city), and soon after was followed up with a visit to the Research, Planning and Analysis Bureau within the Police Department. This resulted in an intensive drilling down into the problem, researching all past calls to the problem area/family identified, and seeking new avenues of inquiry. In a short period of time a clearer picture of people, place and events emerged. Analysis provided information, allowing a proposed and sustainable solution to the existing problem. The decision was made to include a number of public/private resources in the proposed solution. At the end of the day, an in-depth analysis of the problem and subsequent planning and actions that were taken, resolved repeat offending. The officer, a former naysayer, became an ambassador of CPOP, conducted training, motivated others and extensively used the tools available to make this approach to policing successful. It began with a clear discussion about the Chief's purpose of implementing the program and seeing how the police could become more than 911 call responders, sometimes returning to the same location time after time. The vision was clear, the outcome a mirror image of that projection.

EXAMPLE:

Jim was recently promoted to sergeant and was assigned to a group whose reputation for independence and resistance to change was well known. One of his tasks was to have officers under his supervision comply more closely with the department's mission and Chiefs vision. His initial response was to include the staff assigned to him in discussions about work related matters within mission and vision. He thought this would allow a give and take to work decisions as well.

Not only did the group not change, they became more resistant to change and it was difficult to obtain any concessions from them. Feelings of self-worth plummeted with the Sergeant and in consultation with another person he respected within the chain of command; a new path was selected to deal with the aberrant staff.

Jim called a section meeting with all hands and established the following:

- He clearly explained the mission and vision and discussed how they applied to the organization and to each individual. He asked for questions, examples of what they meant to each employee, and identified discrepancies.

- He established his vision of where he saw this group in the next few weeks and months, the benefits of positive change, how each individual and the group would be able to achieve new goals that would enhance all members.

- He explained his role as a supervisor and the expectations he was charged with accomplishing within this role.

- He provided his philosophy of being a supervisor as it pertained to meeting the organization's mission, vision, values and goals.

- He said that in the week ahead he and others in the work group would examine the mission and put it in terms of what their role and responsibilities demanded. He wanted them to ground their job to the mission and determine how they intended to comply. He said the same process would be done with vision, values, goals and objective.

- He explained how he would evaluate overall individual performance including each individual's attendance and engagement at meetings and their level of involvement with him, including personal meetings, individual and group communications and constructive work related feedback.

- He advised that there would be regular meetings to examine work related influences and to conduct short-term planning for work related duties.

- He said that he would maintain a log on each individual to allow a track record of positive and less positive events so at the end of the year, during the annual evaluation, the report would be accurate.

- He further stated that if there was any question or lack of understanding about the previous statements, they were to ask for clarification. By placing individual responsibility he overcame their diversion of engaging in making appropriate changes.

Greensboro, NC Police Chief
Ken Miller

- He shared that he was going to hold them accountable for their performance by having each of them sign a "letter of understanding" of the eight (8) points just made (which he had typed up and passed out as he was making this statement), right then, or to have it signed, dated and returned to him within the next three days.

- He closed with the statement that he considered it his job and a privilege to be available and to assist people to be successful in their positions.

Vision the Pathway to Change.

Vision is often seen as a statement by the CEO and a collection of words that often have little to no meaning to employees. Many employees consider it the Chief, Sheriff, or Superintendent's words that he or she wants to express, but are seldom operationalized.

Vision leads the path forward as it equates to employee behavior and resulting performance. What employees do in carrying out their job duties, the manner in which they provide service, deal with citizen needs and complaints, and meet expectations is contained in the vision and mission of the agency. Deviation from that path forward requires adjustment and effort to resume approved work interaction.

What Can Be Done

1. Insure that people who report to you understand the organization's mission, vision, value, goals and objectives and that they can put them into context with the work they do. Once a vision is formulated, it must be shared across the organization. A written vision is important, but the leader must also conduct a face-to-face meeting to answer questions, to explain how the vision will help the agency grow, move forward and provide benefits to the employees.

2. Spending time with employees to demonstrate and explore how their daily life and the things they do within their job responsibilities can fit within the CEO's vision, is a critical action that enhances the transfer of knowledge and motivates practice. Discuss realistic scenarios or actual events and ask how well they fit with the agency's mission. Work to correct discrepancies and to improve understanding. This helps people adjust to change and to see where they fit within the organizational structure and how the company can and will impact them on a daily basis.

3. Employees need the opportunity to see how the vision fits with what they do. This is not done in a vacuum; rather it emerges from insight, mission, service needs and customer satisfaction. Meet with individual employees as needed and maintain a schedule to insure periodic face-to-face meetings.

4. Supervisors should work one-on-one with each of their subordinates to insure that the mission is known, understood, and that applications to above normal standards are achieved. This actually necessitates spending time with the employee in their work space, performing with them, side by side, exactly what their work duties are, observing application, making corrections if needed and fielding questions.

5. Work closely with those who resist change and help direct them forward toward compliance. Steady insistence and working in collaboration with each resistant employee, seeking their ideas and feedback regarding the change they are resistant to, can be an effective and positive model. Refrain from "giving orders" whenever possible or forcing the individual to change. Begrudging compliance is hardly the goal you want to achieve.

6. Leave nothing to chance. It may require multiple attempts to bring about change, but that is the job at hand. It is not an employee "option" as to whether they make necessary changes toward compliance, higher performance expectations, product delivery, customer satisfaction or the like. It is a necessity that all employees be helped toward change in such a manner as to increase internal motivation, self-worth, a realization that they are an important member of a collaborative team whose individuals each have a voice, but a voice that is for the greater good and that meets the mission, vision, values, goals and objections of the organization.

7. Keep a written record on each person you supervise to maintain an accurate account of work performance. Attempting to recall previous months work is not possible with any degree of accuracy.

8. From the beginning, make it clear you are addressing performance improvement, an area that management is well within its rights to focus on. This reduces appeal to the Union or other group, if resistance is offered.

Write your example.

Questions to consider.

1. How do you gather feedback from your employees as to how they comply and understand the organizations vision?

2. How do you insure that employee work practices are within the mission of the organization?

3. Which of the eight "What can be done" statements do you use?

4. What personal characteristics or traits do you find working well to get an employee to meet compliance requirements?

9. Leaders navigate cultures and motivate people.

An organization's administrative staff is charged with addressing the environment and diversity issues, insuring the development of strategies to manage its culture:

> *"To establish a coordinated strategy to ensure the organizational subcultures are managed in a fashion that encourages incorporating the department's mission and values that impact diversity into the subcultures acceptable attitudes and behavioral standards."*

We are a multi-cultural world and there are not many reasons for excluding anyone based on color, religion or other identifying characteristics. Yet many open and tacit examples of exclusion or shunning occur daily for many reasons, most known only to the person who carries out the act.

Conversely, leadership carries an additional burden of requiring the individual to bury his or her preferences to do what is expected, to act honorably and to achieve mission and goal demands without conflict brought on by prejudicial behavior. This requires supervisor attention to conflict and to mediate any internal struggles that may occur. They must be dealt with quickly and with sustainable solutions emerging from the effort.

> Leaders are not just reflective images of themselves.
>
> They must put aside their personal preferences and conduct the work of the organization.

Knowledge and understanding help bridge conflict points as the individual draws on his or her experience, new information and apply a variety of deductive reasoning techniques to make good decisions and provide direction when needed. What allows this process to take place expeditiously is a high level of knowledge that leads to broad based understanding. When we are dealing with cultural differences, our ignorance is a limiting factor. We also find it more difficult to motivate people when the trigger mechanisms are not understood, which can also limit our choices of action.

EXAMPLE:

Peter's father was a member of the Ku Klux Klan (KKK), as such; he constantly heard the entire diatribe about members of African American race, in terms less than endearing. Peter's older brother followed the father's prejudicial beliefs. His mother looked the other way and never discussed it with them. It was generally known that his Uncles were of the same ilk as his father. It was confusing and made him uneasy to sit and listen to the hate and negativity, but he refused to believe it all and opted to determine things for himself.

After high school, Peter completed two years of criminal justice education at a local community college, applied for a job with the local police department and was hired. Basic police school spent considerable time discussing ethics and integrity and examining scenarios of hate, prejudice, and differences in races, cultural beliefs and philosophy. Policy was clear: police officers were not to treat people differently because of their racial or cultural differences.

Once on patrol, Peter became aware of the subtle yet existing level of bias and prejudice with some of the officers he worked with. There was some joking between officers, but it was somewhat controlled or "hidden" as it violated policy to engage in this type of discussion. What he also noticed was careful, but nonetheless focused attention by some officers on particular people. It might include race, sexual preference, occupation, life-style and other identified differences that some took offense to. In their role as a police officer, the opportunity to make choices and utilize discretion in courses of action is many. All police officers use discretion and most can tell stories about how a person who might have received a warning was in fact ticketed because of what they said, how they looked, talked or acted.

Peter noticed that some officers would issue a citation or make an arrest with a particular type of individual, representing some prejudice, while others not of that persuasion were not charged. On occasion he witnessed subtle but real use of force that was not warranted. It might include putting handcuffs on tighter than necessary, pushing someone to the ground more forcefully than normal, when making an arrest. Peter could see a pattern of this happening to people the individual officer harbored some prejudice against.

On occasion he would ask why the officer did what he or she did, and typically would receive the response as if it were standard officer or agency practice or general information. Never did Peter approach a supervisor to tell on the abusive officers, it just was not done. Six years passed and Peter was promoted to Sergeant and assigned a shift that contained many of the officers he had been concerned about given their previous years' behavior with minorities, gays, prostitutes, youth, drug dealers, users and others who were outside the mainstream of society. The issues that previously had been of concern were now his to address, or so he thought. Years of prejudice and behavior that was in violation of policy, but ignored. The thought that crossed his mind was, now that I'm in a position of authority and leadership, what do I do now?

What Can Be Done

1. Familiarization with policy and law was the first order of business. Future actions had to be based on what is allowable and within proper bounds.

2. Understand the background and causes of aberrant behavior that emerge from beliefs that are grounded in prejudice and bias toward others for what they represent. This means: drill down, determine relevant information, get facts and understand what drives and motivates individual behavior.

3. For similar reasons, learn as much as you can about people who have a different perspective, belief system, racial and personal behavior and lifestyle that is identifiable in order to achieve greater understanding. Knowledge helps with understanding and in turn informs subsequent actions.

4. Individual bias and prejudice are not the only forces at work that direct personal behavior. Organizational sub-cultures are also powerful influences on people. We all know stories of adhering to behavior because others we work with or for, expect it. Expectations by the group are powerful motivators to how we act. While we might disagree, we keep such counsel to ourselves for fear of being ostracized.

5. Be clear with your staff on expectations and how you will work with them to achieve the organization's mission and goals and for them to be successful in this framework. Being upfront, clear and responding to questions early into your new role will go far to prevent future barriers and problems.

6. When you identify an issue, address it quickly. Act on information with thoroughness of exploration. This reduces the potential of the typical "knee-jerk" reactions that occur without the required forethought, careful planning and investigation that such situations/reports call for.

7. Consult with the individual of your attention, discuss motivations and reasons, and ask for input on what they want to do to improve the situation. Agree on a list of proposed changes, establish a timetable and keep in contact to insure that changes are occurring.

8. Work with others in your organization to bring about consistency of behavior within the organization's mission, vision, values, goals and objectives. Ignoring issues, hoping for the best, or waiting for someone else to fix a problem does not work. The responsibility rests with the individual supervisor, you, and it is your responsibility to act immediately when you become aware that involvement is warranted.

You can plug in examples and situational conditions from your place of employment, volunteer group, or other group associations where common goals are known, etc. The key point being: engage in a serious and well-intended manner where appropriate and sustainable change is the identified goal by taking responsibility to work hard to make it happen.

Write your example.

Questions to consider.

1. How do you reconcile cultural differences with your staff and their work related activities?

2. How do you change staff attitudes when obvious bias or other tensions are displayed?

3. How do you handle conflict with staff members, given there are a range of options available to someone in a leadership position.

10. Leaders provide honest feedback.

Honesty, more often than not, is a rare presence in workplace relationships. We skirt issues, hope for the best, overlook minority violations, fear reprisal and either tolerate or overlook inappropriate attitudes and behaviors rather than provide honest feedback or report the problem concern(s).

Supervisors who do not act on the obvious issues are not doing what they were hired to do for the organization. Guided by policy, rules, procedures and practices, performance is easy to manage. When even just one employee engages in attitudinal, behavioral or performance misconduct, and continually does so after colleagues witness and report it, then discipline should start with the supervisor themselves. Why? For failure to perform one of the most important aspects of their jobs: immediate investigation, fact gathering, observation and honest discussion with the employee engaging in the misconduct.

Employee performance and behavior is affected by disagreement and controversy in the workplace.

Resolution of issues is deemed of critical importance to bring the organization back to balance.

We can realign and bring harmony to the work group by addressing issues when they arise. I'm not talking about taking a knee-jerk approach, but first gathering requisite information, determining a course of action and then taking action. The goal is to maintain balance, harmony and to help keep worker morale high and personal performance and attitude in balance. Employees who passively or actively rebel against the company's mission, core values and expectations create problems for everyone at the work site. The longer a problem persists without intervention or corrective action, the greater the disruption. Long term dissonance can rapidly erode all manner of attitude and behavior and create anger, mistrust and reduced performance. All of these are things that are difficult to recover from.

Paula Peters (2000) offered seven concepts for providing employees honest feedback on the work they do and their performance.[9] While uncomfortable, it is within the supervisor's role and responsibility, and it is best to respond

---

[9]. Peters, P. (2000). Seven tips for Delivering Performance Feedback. Bell & Howell Information and Learning Company. http://www.drgnyc.com/list_serve/July14_2003.htm

quickly and directly for the individual and for the organization. The goal is employee growth and development, acquisition of personal responsibility and the overall well-being of the organization. The seven "tips" include:

1. Create the right setting. In privacy, allow no interruptions, both parties turn off cell phones and other devices. Give your full attention to the employee; be clear and concise and as relaxed as possible so the exchange is comfortable.

2. Utilize Self-Feedback. Ask the employee to provide feedback on their performance, to indicate strengths and where improvement might take place. Ask the employee for his or her opinion and listen to what they say without interruption. Follow-up questions are asked at the end of each segment. Give your opinion after the employee has spoken and then ask questions to elicit further information. Offer suggestions and point out what you, as the supervisor, are seeing. Make it a positive exchange.

3. Address Performance Problems Honestly and Directly. Do not let performance issues linger with the "hope" they will improve. Your job is not as a fortune teller, it is to supervise people. Serious issues must be addressed then and there, not in the presence of others, but in a private session. When you have stated what you want the employee to know and be aware of, ask him or her to repeat it so you are sure it is understood. And, do not council an employee based on the rumors of others, see it yourself, have first-hand knowledge and prevent the chance the story you have is not right.

4. Communicate Expectations Clearly. When you provide coaching or instructions, you cannot assume the employee is getting the same message you are providing. Interpretation can vary and will. It is important to be clear, give example or illustration and ask questions to determine if the response indicates understanding. Say what you mean and mean what you say; a rule that has good foundation is reaching the expected goals.

5. Include the Positive. It is not just about the negative. Focusing only on just the inappropriate aspects of the situation will eventually have negative outcomes. Tell employees when positive and good performance is observed, praise for work well done. If the employee is working to make improvements, make note and tell the person of your observation.

6. Make Frequent Feedback. If you conduct just an annual evaluation and attempt to do so from memory, you are not fulfilling your job duties. Speak to employees at the time you observe something either positive or negative, make note of it in your notebook and recognize that work is produced daily, the accumulation of which is next to impossible to remember over the long haul.

7. Keep Documentation. As stated elsewhere in this document, keep notes on each employee to allow accuracy and a running tally, eliminating your reliance on memory only when it comes time for formal evaluation. Check with the organization's human resources department for details on what is acceptable and what is not.

EXAMPLE:

Paul had the annoying habit of asking the guys he worked with to cover for an hour while he met with his girlfriend. He would remain in the immediate vicinity should it become necessary to rush back, but nonetheless making it clear for his colleague to call only in an emergency. Initially, the other guys on the shift did not mind but, over time, and with more requests, his colleagues grew more anger and frustrated with his behavior.

The guys on the shift would complain to each other but not to the supervisor. Eventually tension was noticed by the supervisor. When she inquired further and heard about the entire situation, she became angry at the others for not telling her when the problem began. Her emotional response further increased the separation of people on the shift as everyone, except for the offending party, now felt disconnected. The supervisor's boss got wind of the issues and called her in to discuss what could be done.

How would you act if this was your problem to manage?

Supervisor Musts

1. Be attentive to your employees.
2. Let them know your position, values and expectations. No guessing!
3. Keep careful records.
4. Schedule occasional meeting with each employee.
5. Resolve problems before they gain momentum.
6. Ask employee how they will contribute to positive change and productivity, follow-up and work with them to make it happen.
7. Keep open communications with your employees and supervisors – no surprised, no lapse in timely information as it harms working relationships.

What Can Be Done

    1. It starts with the supervisor's boss who must make clear his or her expectations of the supervisor in how they manage their employee group and the general performance expectations. There should be no doubt about what is expected, how those expectations will be monitored and the rationale as to why.

2. The shift supervisor needs to be more attentive to what is going on and not be so distanced that days pass until a problem becomes observed or communication is clearly made/received. This means being present, talking with others, observing and asking questions.

3. Maintain a journal on each person working for you. Do not rely on memory for details that may need recall weeks or months later. This becomes especially important when someone challenges the supervisor about the details and facts surrounding the dispute. There are also positive outcomes to keeping a daily journal (or log), as the annual evaluation will be much easier to complete with data to revisit.

4. When a problem is sufficiently understood, act immediately. Call the offending person to a meeting, lay out the facts, ask what he or she will do to change the situation and add further details as necessary to insure behavior alteration occurs.

5. Establish follow-up meetings to discuss progress, adjust if needed, and discuss other issues that are also present.

Write your example.

***

Questions to consider.

1. When faced with a challenge, what style of leadership works best for you?

2. Do different situations require different types of leader approach? If yes, provide an example.

3. Do you document conversations with an employee for purposes of recall at a later date? What is your purpose for doing that, if you do?

11. Leaders guide people in doing things right and correcting unacceptable performance and attitudes.

If you see it and are aware of a problem, fix it! Waiting and hoping it will repair itself avoids conflict and conundrum, but it does little to develop your staff. We all grow weary of continuing employee problems and would prefer they do not exist. Life is a series of straight roads with an occasional speed bump, with some time spent straddling the ditch. But, most of it being straight forward.

Accepting the rank and role of a supervisor means you agree to address all manner of employee needs. Most employees meet expectations and do what they are directed to accomplish, but there are also times when some guidance and direction is needed. At those moments, the role of the supervisor and the value of the human condition means you act with compassion, a willingness to help, and a firm commitment to bring about positive change.

Routine often brings complacency. We become comfortable in doing those things that are not stressful, feel good, do not demand engagement in disagreement and form a desire and expectation that things will not change. That's nice, if it can be done, but generally is not a reality. We tend to believe that any ripple in a workplace is deemed unacceptable, but it most certainly is part of organizational life. There will be problems from time to time, there will be individuals who require more attention on occasion, and there will be a time when intervention is needed. It is during those times when supervisors rise to the occasion, step up to the plate, determine what is taking place, gather accurate information and develop a strategy to bring about corrective action. We should note that corrective action may not imply a negative approach to problem solving.

EXAMPLE:

Rebecca was a second shift supervisor at the state's central prison. She supervised eight correctional officers who worked in a unit housing 30 inmates. After receiving two telephone calls from one of her staff that he would be late reporting for duty, she made a mental note to speak with him if it occurred again. She was aware that his demeanor had changed, he seemed more quiet than usual, did not engage in discussion with anyone unless necessary, and appeared disinterested in work related events. While she was curious about these subtle changes, she did observe that he did his work. Performance issues, other than being late, were not on the radar.

60

The employee called in sick a couple of times. As he had sufficient sick leave available, there was no recourse for action, nor did the supervisor feel any discussion was warranted. The slightly different demeanor continued for several weeks. One day the employee did not appear for duty nor had he called out sick. The second morning of no show and no call, an attempt was made to make contact by telephone. That being unsuccessful, someone went to his house and got no response. Through normal safety procedures and calls, a police officer ended up going to his home, only to discover that he had committed suicide using a shotgun.

The supervisor was devastated and engaged in self-blame for not taking more aggressive action when it was initially brought to her attention that this employee was observed to be acting slightly different than usual. An internal investigation disclosed that the employee's wife had suddenly announced she was leaving after 30 years of marriage, without any previous warning or indicators. The employee had not shared this information with any of his peers and as time passed his obsession and disquiet increased. Alone with his thoughts he made the decision to commit suicide.

We can second guess all manner of scenario about what should or could have been done, but to do so generally, accomplishes little of substance. Should the supervisor have spoken to the employee early on when awareness of personality changes and engagement level were noticed? Certainly, as that is what the supervisor's role and responsibilities allow. The question for you, the reader, is what would you have done in this scenario?

What Can Be Done

1. Do not become office bound. Supervisors who are content within the walls of their office miss much of what their responsibility dictates they should be aware of. Walls keep people out and isolate the supervisor from activities occurring outside of his or her sight.

2. Stop being absorbed in the process and busy tasks and take the time to get out there, look around and listen. What are your people actually doing in their work environment? Talk with them, spend time, observe and learn of issues, needs, ideas and suggestions. Engage in problem-solving and resolving issues.

3. When you become aware of an issue do not react until you have investigated and obtained relevant facts. Quick action taken rashly causes a worsening situation to emerge. When facts are known, arrange for a private meeting with the individual if that is the case, to discuss what is known and to seek solutions.

4. As a supervisor, your primary role is to align employees under your charge with the organization's mission and to insure that performance and use of resources are being directed in that quest. You need not do it harshly or seek to intimidate the person into compliance, as it works best and lasts longer if agreement and motivation toward a willingness to change is obtained. A collaborative discussion opens many possibilities.

5. It is important to listen to your individual employees. When all the talk is done and a solution is proposed, establish a follow-up meeting to check progress and discuss how the individual feels about what is taking place. Make adjustments as needed.

6. Once a plan is in place, measure compliance and progress, adjust as needed and conduct follow-up review and meetings to insure that attitude and behavior changes are occurring.

Write your example.

Questions to consider.

1. When you consider your role with people you supervise, how do you see it? Are you organization, person or a combination focused?

2. Is your work day filled with busy stuff or are you among the people you supervise? This goes to value placement.

3. How would your employees describe you? What are the major traits they find positive and helpful to them?

12. Leaders assist people to examine their future and assist them with career development.

Work (next to family) is often the most important aspect of our lives. While we work to receive wages, we also invest ourselves beyond fulfilling the duties assigned to us. When we seek to identify ourselves it is often by stating what we do, where we work or some association to a profession or field of practice.

While focus is on getting the job done, there are many parallel practices to consider whose focus is on the individual and his or her growth, well-being and future success. Not to do that is to infer less value to the person who has committed giving of one's skills, knowledge, talent, time and energy to the organization.

We also know that not all people are motivated to excel and reach lofty positions, some being content to report to work, do what they are hired to do, and at the end of the day leave it behind until tomorrow. However, the focus of this assertion is on the leader and his or her responsibility to assist employees under their oversight to grow and become the best that they can be.

Leaders must be aware of the current conditions of the work, what the future is likely to bring and to determine how the "here and now" will fit to the "then and there" and make plans to bring the organization and the employees along on that journey. To not plan or engage in future discovery and preparation is to linger on the path of inertia, which ultimately will diminish overall growth and result in an uninspired organization.

Assisting people with career development is dependent on several factors. They are:

- Knowing each employees strengths, weaknesses, interests, motivations and aspirations.

- Share with them the organization's present condition and where it appears to be headed.

- Discuss what new skills and abilities will be needed and inquire if they have interest in obtaining them for future growth within the organization.

- Learn from them their thoughts and ideas on how they want to fit within the organization and what their aspirations are.

- Discuss how they can accomplish new goals, what must be done, what their role is and how you, as supervisor, can assist.

- Draft a plan that you both agree on and then support them as they seek to implement it. Not everything can be accomplished, but honest attempts can and should be made.

- Keep track of steps taken to change and grow. Relying on memory is insufficient and a notebook or file is acceptable. The more distant details are difficult to bring forward, thus a written record works best.

- Advocate for your people.

- Maintain open communication: listen, respond and seek to be inclusive.

- Be a trustworthy person, honor confidences and be honest in your dealing with employees in all you do.

We often become absorbed in the job, the work at hand, and forget that the prime responsibility is to the people who are working to fulfill the mission. We cannot ignore them and should put that function as a high priority. Well trained and engaged employees will make the work outcomes all the better.

EXAMPLE:

Bill had a large family. The costs associated with them precluded his attending college or seeking additional training to improve his marketability or promotion within the organization. His work record was impeccable, no lost work days, not a complainer, got along well with everyone and offered to help if additional time was needed on a project. He fit well within the organization and although he was considered hard working, he largely went unnoticed.

Due to promotions, a new supervisor, Catherine, was assigned to Bill's Unit. After a few months on the job she observed the positive traits stated about Bill and decided to learn more and to inquire why he was not seeking promotions or higher level jobs. She arranged a meeting with Bill to explore her observations and to make these inquiries.

During the meeting Catherine more clearly learned to understand the strength and depth of Bill's character, his many skills, his humbleness and solid work ethic, and his deep seated wish to be able to obtain education and move forward within the organization. She left the meeting feeling inspired by the person Bill was and by the skills and level of motivation he possessed. Catherine took the liberty to develop a draft of a plan that would help Bill to gain the additional training and experience necessary to move him further on his dreamed of career path.

Catherine set up a second meeting with Bill after presenting her ideas and information about Bill to her manager and received the stamp of approval to move forward with her plan. She met with Bill and explained how impressed she had been with Bill's history, skills and work ethic, and how, from this, she had presented a plan to management and received support in moving forward. She explained to Bill that to do so, he would need to review and edit the plan based upon what he felt was comfortable and realistic for himself in moving forward, if he was so interested. Included in the plan were the basic steps and resources available to help him achieve these goals. Bill agreed to review the materials and to make notes and changes on the draft, and to meet with Catherine the following week. Bill left this meeting with a level of excitement and self-worth unlike anything he had ever experienced in his professional working career.

It is important to note that Catherine and Bill will have plan adjustments to consider as they move forward. However, the ease of their discussions and the openness of information shared, past and present would make that process easier as they continued along this path.

What Can Be Done

1. You assist each employee by entering into a discussion specifically scheduled for the purpose of which will be defined before the first meeting occurs (Note or direct communication with the employee, such as "Bill, I'd like to meet with you on Tuesday from 1-2 p.m. to talk about your positive work history with us and about your future goals.").

2. You must be informed, work from factual information, maintain an open mind and be willing to listen.

3. Ask questions to fill in unknown information. No decisions should be made in haste and without full knowledge. Where appropriate, drill down to get below the surface to "leave no stone unturned" as it were. It is not about future embarrassment it is about the fullness of understanding on which you base your decisions.

4. Do not make any promises that cannot be fulfilled. If doubt exists seek to find answers and if unsuccessful, say so.

5. Reach agreement through discussion and inquiry. Be open and honest at all times.

6. Put the final agreement on paper and determine measurable outcomes or check points that will be used to determine how well the plan is unfolding.

7. Make course corrections with the other party; do not operate in isolation or from a position of power. It is not about you!

8. Keep your superiors informed so they do not err in making a counter decision due to ignorance on their part.

9. Meet the employee on a scheduled basis to review progress, answer questions, identify and resolve problems, and keep track of progress.

10. Respect confidences where necessary. Mutual trust is the only bond worth 100 percent surety.

Write your example.

Questions to consider.

Questions to consider.

1. Are you confident that employees under your supervision are performing at their highest level and well versed in the organization's mission, vision, values and goals?

2. When coaching employees are you focused on their growth and development as well as the organizations?

3. Would you describe your leadership style as helpful and caring or more direct and getting the job done? Why have you chosen these or other styles?

13. Leaders stretch to the positive and recognize that mistakes occur. They help individuals overcome future error.

No one is infallible, and as hard as we try not to, we occasionally make mistakes. Much of life is situational, meaning we are not in control of every move and we are unable to anticipate what might be harmful to a great idea and well developed plan. There are too many moving variables to insure that everyone is accounted for and adequate cover in place to protect against negative input.

Most of the time it is business as usual and few bumps appear. An occasional pot hole appears and some are able to maneuver around it, while others hit it, curse its presence, and condemn the road crews for not fixing it.

> Recognizing good performance, helps reduce tension when correction is needed.

Other that expending a bit of hot air, little was accomplished in the rant. We often resort to complaining at work about conditions or policy that we do not like and like the pot hole it will probably be there tomorrow. We do not engage in a depth of problem solving that will determine sustainable solutions to those things that are frustrating and disruptive.

Stretching to the positive means we are aware of information that is known and which will allow appropriate action to be taken. Calling the highway department and relaying information about the hole may get it fixed that day. Driving down the road swearing at unknown and unseen people, while it feels good, accomplishes nothing. This same analogy in other aspects of work or personal endeavors reaches the same conclusion.

At work, be aware of the little and big things your staff does that is positive. We come to expect good work by employees and never mention it or give praise. We leap on a negative outcome and rush in to fix the problem and sometimes throw the employee under the proverbial bus. Again, an example of an uncalled for over-reaction. Recognizing the many good things employees do and comparing that against a single misdeed, tempers response and does not destroy employee and supervisor role and position. Stretching toward the good also feels better for the occasional time when you must engage in a negative discussion, it will be with knowledge of that person's value and feelings. A much more positive step!

Dunstan self-describes himself as someone who 'drove cattle' all his life. He worked on various cattle ranches across the southwest for the past 50 plus years, living mostly on the range, a sleeping bag, a dependable horse and a group chuck wagon for coffee and food. He was content with that lifestyle as it fit his self-image and expectations. He wanted for little, had little, expected even less and did what he was asked to do without complaint.

Lately, he thought it would be nice to have a more comfortable bed to sleep in, a roof over his head when it rained or snowed and perhaps a less strenuous lifestyle given he was well into his 60s. One night during a thunderstorm he dozed while sitting on his horse and the cattle wandered away toward a dry river bed, which with all the rain might result in a fast flood roaring through. The ranch foreman happened to be awake and rode out to check on the cattle and Dunstan. Finding the cattle nowhere in sight and both Dunstan and his aging horse standing idle, both sleeping, the first reaction was one of anger. Looking at Dunstan, he saw a man who asked for little and who never complained and someone who was tired. He rode up to Dunstan and spoke quietly saying he could use his help to find the cattle.

When all returned to normal, the foreman asked Dunstan if he might be interested in taking a job at the ranch, one that would keep him under cover, dry quarters, dining hall, and a less 'round the clock' schedule. Dunstan said he would consider it asking for time to mull it over.

At the later meeting, Dunstan said he would like that offer but felt guilty for even being considered. The foreman simply said, "Dunstan you have lived your life on the range, seen many things, worked in heat and cold, rain and sunshine, hard times and good and perhaps he had more to offer in the new position that neither of them had considered". Dunstan smiled in his shy way, shook hands and looked toward a new endeavor, self-pride in place and thankful for the opportunity.

Sometimes an event will occur and if we take a moment to not just react and think more broadly, we may be given insight that turns out to be the right course of action. But, we first have to realize that opportunities do happen and when they happen, to be ready to take the right step forward.

What Can Be Done

1. Do not let your emotions over rule common sense. Focusing too closely on an event and not looking left, right, up and down to see what else might be learned, restricts your ability to make the correct decision.

2. Unless other reasons substantiate a particular response, take a moment to consider what the situation provides to help you learn and broaden your options. A myopic view may not provide the best set of details on which to make a decision.

3. Talk with employees to get their input and hear their stories. You will be amazed what will be learned that has useful application to the welfare of both the employee and the organization.

4. Spend time considering the needs of the organization and see what employees match up and would fit symbiotically for the benefit of both.

5. When a mistake happens, take time to discuss it with the employee to find ways to avoid future repeat occurrences. A one-time mistake is also a good learning opportunity. Obviously is the same mistake is made several times a different strategy is necessary.

6. Talk with other supervisors and learn of common mistakes that are taking place and examine if additional training is needed, a change in policy or procedure, and explore tactics that can be taken to improve the situation. It may not be only a people problem, rather organizational influences that require adjustment.

Write your example.

Questions to consider.

1. How would you describe your reaction to a stressful situation?

2. When an employee makes a misstep, is your first reaction to chew him or her out, or do you choose a more tempered approach?

3. Do you describe yourself as someone who helps others, or who prefers to hold them accountable to fulfill their responsibilities with little intervention?

14. Leaders provide a blend of balance and good management.

When it comes to leadership, we easily get trapped in a one-size fits all model for managing and supervising people. We are conscious of the rank and role and see ourselves as a quasi-leader of sorts, often struggling to reconcile job responsibilities with employee relationships. It need not be this way. Supervisors are leaders who must represent the organization and what it stands for and believes in. As such, we must act, personally and professionally, in a way that allows employee inclusion, rejecting the attitude of "us vs. them," or confrontational when it comes to working with all employees. Leaders are concerned with the feelings, attitudes, and performance of employees, making sure that the work performance and attitude of each employee fits with the organization's mission, vision, values and goals. Alignment with mission and goals is the organization's expectation; after all, each employee is being paid to achieve them!

Employees may have a personal vision of their work that does not match with the organization's expectations. This must be recognized (by you, as the supervisor), and fixed! One of the first important steps is to talk about the mission and goals and to help people see how their work fits within those items, to resolve any problems they have in perception, understanding or attitude, and to assist each employee in aligning with their position and performance expectations. Align people and work. It is not about the individual but they can be helped to see the larger picture. By beginning on day one, during orientation, via the review of the company's mission and goals, and then assessing each employee's understanding of same, you begin to plant the seed of understanding. The seed analogy recognizes that each individual is a part of something greater than themselves; meaning the organization itself.

It is important that the leader consistently and clearly presents the organization's expectations in regard to the critical need for the employee to be aligned with them. Doing so requires the leader to model this blending of self, position and work performance expectations with the mission and goals. Beyond the need for the leader to be in the forefront in representing what the organization expects of all employees is the need for the leader to join with the employee as part of the work force.

What does this mean? It means that the leader is in the field or workspace connecting with each and every employee, in some capacity. Doing so opens the door and lays the foundation for communication and relationship building. The leader should be communicating a genuine level of concern and interest in each employee: concern for their health, their welfare, their thoughts, feelings, ideas, and recommendations, along with their personal and professional views of their position within the organization.

Most all jobs have some flexibility to allow the employees and supervisors to work collaboratively to develop procedures and strategies that are within the framework of the mission and goals. As the leader, it is critical to create a culture of openness, inclusiveness and collaboration. If the organization expects each employee to be a part of the whole, then it is only fair for each employee to be shown the interest and respect due to them as workers and human beings. If a leader shows this interest and opens themselves up to each employee, they set the stage for a higher level of commitment and worker satisfaction, as well.

> **"As a leader, you must accept responsibility for your role in the culture. You are the chief role model and trust builder, and people look to your behavior and decisions for guidance on their own behavior and decision making"**
> (Situational Leadership: Balance of Leadership Style And Readiness (E), 2009[i]).

Leaders should not expect their position to be a virtual "piece of cake." To do so would result in failure in the position. We are dealing with people who are working within a framework of an organization's policy and procedures and the occasionally well understood mission and goals. Supervisors (Leaders) who are concerned for both the organization and the employee and work to keep them both in harmony. And, with an ever watchful eye on the third party aspect of the customer, will assist in maintaining a more harmonious work environment, overall.

EXAMPLE:

Police are traditional in their beliefs about how the job should be done. Law enforcement is the preferred descriptive for what they do and they are not prone to accept deviation from that vision. For decades, enforcement has been seen as the way to control crime and criminals and to make the community a safer place. The prevailing attitude is, make enough arrests and jail enough bad guys and the community is a safer place.

Numerous variations of this model have been introduced to modify how the job is carried out, to bring it closer to the community, and to increase effectiveness and efficiency. Most have failed, while the organization of policing resumes its former perspective and delivery of services. Employee selection, training and the emerging culture often resists change. Unions and formal work associations further add to the resoluteness to hold tight in the face of change.

Community problem oriented policing seeks to bridge the semi-closed police role within the larger community, to create collaboration and partnerships between public and private organizations. This is a major balance challenge, one where the supervisor is in the most critical position to make it happen.

Training supervisors in the model (of community problem oriented policing), and making it crystal clear how the role of community, problem identification, collaboration and problem-solving work symbiotically, is a first step. When change occurs, the organization can expect resistance and doubt to form, rumors to occur and all manner of confusion to result. Therefore, it is imperative that the organization spend sufficient time in educating the supervisors, to explore every question and to provide answers and rationale for why things are taking place. The supervisor will, in turn, have to pass this same information along to the employees. No deviation from the true path must be allowed. If knowledge is present, the transition is smoother. When people are operating from separate and personal perspectives, confusion will occur. As such, training must be carefully planned. When it is, it tends to naturally expand and build further upon itself as the expected response from all employees is more clearly aligned with the model and expectations.

 When the Charlotte-Mecklenburg Police Department made the decision to transition from traditional to community problem oriented policing, it took five years of training and application, review and adjustment. Eventually, habit and practice emerged as the way of life representing organizational philosophy. Supervisors were charged with integrating the mission, vision, values, and goals into the performance standards of each employee. The entire agency focused on the mission and all of the individual efforts were aligned to this activity, which included goals.

As performance deviated from mission and goals, supervisors were expected to discuss how the individual could realign and adopt new procedures that kept them within accepted outcomes. It was a give and take, a discussion and examination of how the old and the new could be accomplished, and where differences could be made compatible.

What Can Be Done

1. Be the leader the organization believes you to be. If you are not sure,

ask someone in higher authority who has the grand vision and understands how employees must function.

2. You represent the organization and are not there to accommodate a diversity of attitudes and feelings. As such, you are expected to align people with policy and expectations within the mission, vision, values and goals.

3. Be open and honest in all your dealings with employees and your boss. Any deviation will eventually lead to problems.

4. Help employees fit their skills, knowledge and abilities to the job. This also means helping them reconcile their personal agenda with the organizations. The organization has the primary right to expect that employee performance aligns with mission, vision, values and goals.

5. The supervisor must be consistent in his or her dealings with employees and the organization. Change occurs as a natural outcome of doing business and it must be managed or it becomes disruptive.

6. Show honest concern for your employees. This means you cannot be successful if you only see them on occasion or when there are issues. You must be engaged with them to know them and then be more easily able to identify when imbalance occurs and quickly work with the employee to achieve balance. And so, get out of your office and spend time with the workers in their environment.

7. Rigidity is harmful in most normal workplaces. Seek a method of flexibility that remains true to the mission, vision, values and goals and to your employees' creativity, skills, knowledge and abilities. Seek to constantly align employees with organization and customer.

8. Communicate and keep open lines to all employees. A break in the line will lead to sub-level discussions of which you are not part. Cultures form and are strong influences on behavior. The way to minimize negative outcomes is to have open discussion and decision-making.

9. Organization and employee balance in fulfilling needs and expectations are not always a natural outcome of being in business. The supervisor must work to make it happen. That is his or her job. The expectation by everyone is that the supervisor (leader) can, and will, handle it.

Industry Example

The following illustrates an important maxim, executives who address work-life balance maintain sustainable and productive employees.

In a recent Hay Group survey of senior executives in companies eligible to participate in *Fortune* magazine's annual rankings of the World's Most Admired Companies, fully 49 percent of respondents from organizations ranked in the top three in their industries in corporate reputation reported that addressing work-life balance issues as a "top priority" or "very important" as a human capital challenge over the next two years.

These results reflect awareness that helping employees achieve a reasonable work-life balance is not just a matter of creating attractive work environments, but also a critical consideration for sustaining performance over time.

We isolated a best-practice group of organizations that scored in the top quartile on employees' ratings of their responsiveness to work-life balance concerns and compared them with organizations scoring in the bottom quartile on this issue, examining a wide range of workplace practices.

The results suggest that organizations need to look beyond programmatic responses. The organizations that are judged by employees to be the most effective in helping employees juggle work and personal responsibilities effectively manage a broader set of workplace dynamics. Specifically, within these "work-life balance leaders:"

- Clear direction regarding organizational priorities is provided, to help employees focus on the highest-value tasks;
- Policies and practices are consistently implemented, to ensure that workloads are seen as fairly and equitably distributed;
- High levels of teamwork within and across organizational units are emphasized, to provide employees with access to support from co-workers in coping with work demands;
- Strong support for training and development and high levels of empowerment are provided, to ensure that employees have the skills and decision-making authority to get the job done; and
- Adequate resources (e.g., tools, equipment and technology) are supplied, to enable employees to execute work tasks efficiently and with high quality.

Write your example.

Questions to consider.

1. When you consider yourself and your work investment, would you say that you are balanced and well-rounded? This goes to how much time and energy you have for others under your direction.

2. How do you help employees realign their performance with organization expectations?

3. Do you consider yourself a good model for employees to follow within the organization?

4. Do you encourage employee workplace engagement through a culture of openness and inclusion?

15. Leaders look after their people.

Leaders take the time and personal attention to nurture and motivate their supervisees in a seriously manner. They set expectations and provide ongoing interaction that includes education, encouragement and corrective feedback. They model a level of collaboration and cooperation between themselves and others, growing the belief of "us and we" vs. "us against them." They create and work to sustain a strong feeling of teamwork.

Promotion, for any individual, is a step up, and a new way of life in the professional realm. With the role comes new responsibility and expectations. Personal accountability first requires acceptance that it is to your shoulders the new demands and expectations have fallen. When good things occur, you will receive praise and when bad happens, you also must accept the negative outcomes as well. Acknowledging that issues exist goes with supervisory responsibility even when it seems unfair or something you really could not control.

> People are critically important to meeting mission and goals—to being part of the product, progress and success of any organization.

The phrase, "*people are our most important product*" refers to the work being done by employees. General Electric once used the phrase, "*progress is our most important product*" with great success to market their products. Organizations cannot operate without a strong employee base. People are critically important to meeting mission and goals—to being part of the product, progress and success of any organization.

As a leader, take responsibility by actively supervising your employees. There are numerous details that must be attended to and at each level of your position and from the perspective of the larger organization. Remember this: no aspect, no detail, is insignificant when it comes to achieving success. To achieve the overall goals and missions of your organization, as a leader you must be actively engaged with each employee as they carry out their duties. You provide guidance and motivation, evaluate outcome measures and help people to excel. Where you actively identify any barriers that might exist, it then becomes your responsibility to find ways to overcome them and keep your focus on doing what is right to achieve these goals, with the help of your team members.

Supervisors must attention to their employees and the jobs they perform. Employee and management/leadership commitment leads to better performance and reduces employee turnover. An attitude that "one size fits all" is highly unlikely to lead to overall organizational success. How well the supervisor relates to each of his or her employees is a factor in how one feels about the place they work. We should value each of our employees and work to make them all proficient within the strengths and abilities they have, thereby insuring they are in alignment with expectations. If not, find solutions and help the employee obtain training or other job enhancements to bring them up to speed. Treat all employees fairly, honestly and openly. Employees, like the supervisor, want to believe they offer value to the organization and the work they perform.

Look for signs that an employee is unhappy or is distracted while working. When behavioral changes are noticeable don't ignore them! Generally, the philosophy of "wait and see" does not achieve the desired changes. The work environment does change and fluctuate, for some it is easy to manage, but for others it can be overwhelming. Be sure to pay attention and to intervene, help and support when it becomes obvious.

Employees who understand their job role and expectations, how it fits within the organization's mission, vision, values and goals are more likely to be successful. If the lack of clear understanding exists, expectations will falter, personal agendas become easier to adopt and friction may gain a foothold. Engaged employees understand their role and are able to make adjustments when conflict occurs. The culture of the organization and the sub-cultures that exist can be at odds if left unattended. Supervisors have the responsibility to understand all positions and to maintain alignment. We must treat all employees with respect and demonstrate that they are a valued member of the organization. To do differently, is to erode a strong relationship, one that is necessary if productivity and well-being are to exist.

We have all heard that people are our most important product and few disagree. The rub comes in when we examine what we do to support that statement. Following initial hire and training and perhaps an orientation period, it is not long before new employees are blending into the culture. For the most part, employee work behaviors quickly become routinized and habit becomes a daily event. Generally, as long as someone is not causing disruption, leaders will allow them to work as they do if they are within general parameters of the organizations mission and goals and meeting performance expectations.

Supervisors, who are not drawn to an employee due to performance problems or outlandish behavior, often maintain a hands-off approach to employee management.

With supervisor workload demands often taking attention from employees to processing paperwork and other management issues, a leader can easily find that their ability to have or make time for hands-on engagement with their supervisees, diminishes. When this pattern of leadership occurs, employees find their own work pace and routines from watching their coworkers and going to them with their questions and concerns instead of their supervisor. If this pattern sounds familiar, it is through frequent occurrence across America. However, smart companies and leaders realize that it is not the best way to run an organization or to meet their company's mission and goals.

As stated previously, expectations must be clearly stated (and often), discussed at length (and repeated often), and the leader must review with each employee, how his or her role and function fit into the organizations

 standards. This is not a one-time only discussion, because as the work changes, as experience increases, as the environment and the organization finds itself changing and evolving, so, too, must the expectations. Having discussed an employee's work, not just at the annual evaluation,

www.designsponge.com

but through repeated formal and information interactions and meetings with each individual or group is a good business practice. It maintains alignment of work, process and outcomes in line with organizational expectations. It provides an opportunity to examine strengths and areas where improvement can be made. It allows the supervisor to inquire if the employee is experiencing any difficulty and if so, to find a solution. Accountability emerges from a collaborative effort by the employee and his or her supervisor who examines the expectations to the work being done and finds solutions to problems.

Supervisors need to keep a notebook and calendar and schedule time with each employee under their supervision. It should be scheduled and the employee informed of what will be discussed and to allow time for the supervisor to be questioned. It is all about keeping the train on the track and in making improvements, encouraging, supporting and being available to listen to issues and needs and getting them fulfilled. Showing concern, being attentive, letting your employees know they are important to you and the organization is a first priority.

Conflict had been building for four months as the union and the organization's management continues to disagree on the latest contract negotiation. The company stated that due to the economy it was very difficult to increase benefits and the size of the pay raise requested. The union said that benefit changes were not the issue. They stated that it was the lack of a pay raise for the past two years, along with rising costs for food, fuel, insurance and other routine quality of life materials, that was making it difficult to provide for daily family needs and maintain an appropriate level of family well-being.

Monica was a third shift supervisor and was well aware of employee dissatisfaction with the negotiations. Being on the third shift and away from the daily fray, there were numerous rumors that ran the gamut of A to Z. Work production was suffering and the effect on employee attitude and morale was noticeably negative. A decision was needed on how Monica would manage the employees on her shift until resolution was obtained between the union and management.

Her first task was to find factual and current information, to be up-to-date, as it were. She did this by talking with the union President and a company Vice President. She advised her staff she was doing this.

Her second step was to ask employees on her shift to meet an hour early one day, not to seek overtime, but to come in to listen to what she learned from her information gathering and meeting(s). At that meeting she requested employee comments and input to allow their thoughts, questions, concerns and needs to be heard. Before conclusion of the meeting, she discussed the need to not engage in pessimistic thinking and she asked them for their patience in waiting it out. She reiterated that nothing good could be gained by furthering the negative gossip and general attitude of antagonism or defiance heard of or seen in other shift staffers. Her third action step was to meet with the union President to share with him, in general terms, what her employees were thinking and feeling. She asked him to keep her informed as not knowing leads to rumor and that was not healthy for anyone. He said he would do so and set up a meeting schedule and communication plan.

As the days went on, her actions kept her shift calm. The workers were comfortable in knowing what they did and in adopting the attitude to wait and see. If questions were asked, Karen found out the correct information and/or passed it along to the appropriate union representative or President. These combined actions were very helpful in many ways.

What Can Be Done

1. With promotion arises a new role and one must prepare to accept all aspects.

2. Acclimate self with role and responsibility.

3. Resolve to be accountable.

4. Value of employees is critical and must be primary role.

5. Supervision is an active process and passivity cannot be allowed.

6. Engage with your employees, get out of your office and be where they work.

7. Provide guidance as needed in the moment-- not tomorrow.

8. Strengthen individual capacity to do the job right.

9. Help individuals overcome barriers.

10. Observe how people interact within the organization and help remove barriers.

11. Work to align employees with the organization.

12. Look for signs of issues and problems and treat symptoms

13. Help people to know mission, vision, values and goals.

14. Work with the organizations culture and sub-cultures for harmony and improvement.

15. Dispel rumors by finding out the truth from the best source available and pass along the information to employees.

16. Remember, organization first or the mission becomes confused and employees with it.

Write your example.

Questions to consider.

1. Ask yourself, if people are critical to the organization's mission, what you do to enhance that outcome.

2. Does the agency provide training and the opportunity for employees to see how what they do contributes to the overall mission?

3. If disconnect appears, how is it addressed and brought up to speed?

4. As a supervisor / leader, how do you reconcile accountability to both employees under your charge and the overall organization?

16. Leaders are proactive and provide time mentoring others to effect positive change.

Transforming people into an organizational posture that signals their willingness and ability to set personal goals that are consistent with the organization, to understand and seek compliance with the mission and values, is a prime responsibility of the supervisor. A transformational leader strengthens employee trust and the supervisor is seen as trustworthy.

Supervisors are charged with the responsibility of teaching other employees as individual needs dictate. You cannot achieve this goal unless you are willing to spend time with employees to understand individual strengths and weakness and to hear from them as they express needs and desires. The supervisor is also a coach, one who informs guides, provides example and seeks resources needed to help each employee become successful.

Moriarty[10] suggests that being proactive in a leadership role demands empowerment, coaching and establishing and maintaining strong performance standards. Providing employees with proper guidance to understand their job, role, and responsibilities, is a complex and demanding aspect of the leader's overall functions. Service and customers are central to this focus as well. If we believe that the employee is a valued commodity, we must include them in decision-making and being part of helping the organization to grow. Proactive leaders are not afraid to include employees, to solicit their input, and to seek honest and direct evaluation of what is being done and how it can be improved.

&)CR

Insure the employee knows his or her job, the role they play, expectations for performance, and how they fit within the organizations mission, vision, values and goals.

&)CB

The second important role of a supervisor is to plan and devote sufficient time with employees to allow their input to work related activities, and to determine what is being done, by whom and how well. When something of a negative nature takes place the supervisor suddenly appears and takes some action to rectify the situation. The time and distance spent with one's employees should be narrowed, making them your first priority. Mentoring and coaching should be considered a positive employee building activity.

---

[10]. Tom Moriarty http://www.alidade-mer.com/Track_4_-_People_Skills_-_Tom_Moriarty_-_Proactive_Leadership_Paper.pdf

We often see supervisors send individuals and groups off to do specific work and find contentment within that narrow scope of their assignment. An example is a supervisor of public works road crews who makes assignments in the morning to fill pot holes, repair sidewalks, clear storm drains, mow intersection grass, run the sweeper over several streets, and numerous other duties. The crews go off and report back at the end of the day. The supervisor attacks the pile of papers on her/his desk and makes follow-up telephone calls. The day slips by and ends. Tomorrow begins in fourteen hours.

One of the first calls of the morning is an irate homeowner who complains that the sweeper ruined several feet of lawn that abuts the street by cutting it too close. The supervisor's first reaction is to drive to the current location of the sweeper and reprimand the employee operating the sweeper. Given time to think about the situation, the supervisor realizes that the sweeper driver was just hired and had not been given proper training on what should be done. The supervisor realized the mistake began with not providing that training and through that process a different attitude emerges.

What Can Be Done

1. Help employees set personal goals that are consistent with the organization's mission and goals.

2. Create an environment of trust. Without that condition supervision becomes a task and does not allow for open exchange, which is critical to resolving issues and building capacity.

3. A supervisor is also a teacher. In that role the supervisor (as teacher) helps with the acquisition and integration of information germane to one's job and responsibilities.

4. Spending time with employees allows the supervisor to actually see what is taking place, to get more in-depth knowledge about them as people and employees, and to determine where assistance, training, coaching and inclusion might be helpful. It also allows the employee greater understanding of the supervisor and to come to expect frequent presence and open exchanges.

5. Coaching is providing guidance, presenting information and resources and helping the employee adopt new concepts, processes and other positive job enhancing help. The coaching role is designed to assist with and support an

employee's continued growth and development within the context of the organization.

6. Solicit input from employees, seek their advice and learn about their knowledge of the organization and how the mission is fulfilled.

7. Carry information learned from those who you supervise to administration, particularly if there is value in what is being shared. This keeps the organization informed and seeing multiple perspectives, not just what they are working on.

Write your example.

Questions to consider.

1. As a transformational leader, how do you strengthen trust between yourself and employees?

2. Describe the ways you spend time with employees to understand their individual strengths and weakness and to determine their needs and desires.

3. Do you engage in coaching helping employees, providing information, offering guidance and solving problems that arise?

4. Explain how you solicit employee input and seek their honest evaluation of what is being done for work, how it can be improved, and then use that information appropriately.

5. Consider how you build trust, what are the positive markers and importantly, maintain that relationship with employees.

17. Leaders align people to future jobs preparing them for new positions and responsibilities.

It is human nature that employees, over time, often become complacent in the work place, not only with the work itself, but with the daily routine and level of performance and position expectations.

Supervisors are not above complacency, either. In fact, they are often complacent in their thinking about their supervisees and performance expectations. In the supervisor's position, habit and conformity rules and this can have the deleterious effect of narrowing one's awareness of people and process. We lose our focus on the day to day performance and efforts of our employees, often missing the big and little effects that are going well, let alone missing the hidden or overt issues of concern or the "red flags" that require our attention. We assume that a lack of reported concerns, problems or complaints is a signal to let well enough alone.

 A broader organizational view will drag us from inertia to action. This includes waking up and becoming more aware of the employees under our responsibility. We need to see and recognize people working for us in a clear and thorough manner. We need to help them maintain the organization's high standards, and engage in personal and professional growth in the workplace via setting goals and objectives for themselves within their position and the larger company[11]. All of these require the interest, support, and ongoing interaction between supervisor and supervisee.

Supervisors should maintain reference records on each employee to provide accurate information and reduce dependence on memory and foggy recollection. Recording information is often construed as a negative activity, done to collect information on the employee, resulting in corrective action associated with problem performance or situations. Data (information) collection can also be for positive purposes as well. As the supervisor gets to know the employee, many details emerge in the course of a work week that are complimentary and should be captured for the employee's record. The importance of this often comes front and center when the annual evaluation is due and supervisors are left with knowledge of the most recent employee events but not able to remember eight, ten or twelve months ago in reference to each specific individual and their performance. Evaluations need

---

[11] [Image] http://www.dreamstime.com/royalty-free-stock-photos-success-knowledge-abilities-skills-image28784628

to reflect accurate details and information that accurately describes each employee's work performance and compliance with the organization's expectations. This single responsibility is probably one of the more important functions of a supervisor.

Supervisors also have the responsibility to match employees with organizational needs, to prepare people for promotion and identify a good fit to new endeavors. Looking ahead to change, growth and revision of duties and services, supervisors should maintain an active matrix of people and positions and anticipate when changes are going to occur. Jobs have identified skills, knowledge and abilities (SKA's) associated with them. Knowing these SKA's, where deficits can be fixed or corrected before the need arises, or a situation becomes critical, enhances promotability. This also helps motivated employees look ahead, plan and seek the organization's support in upgrading and enhancing their personal marketability. This is collaboration between the employee, supervisor and organization and, as such, requires active engagement.

Preparing people for promotion and advancement is an important core responsibility of each supervisor and one of the central charges that benefits both the organization and the individual employee. A chart (matrix) of needed SKA's allows the employee to fill in where they have the assets associated with making a "goodness of fit," in areas where deficits exist.

The information from the matrix, combined with the ongoing information collection for each supervisee, provides a comprehensive data base that assists with acquiring the requisite updating, planning and moving of employees, within the larger organization, into appropriate positions. Seamless transition to new positions should not start with a post-promotion scramble to acquire the right SKA's.

EXAMPLE:

Many emergency 911 centers experience a robust turnover. This is due to high stress, rotating schedules and the lack of perceived organizational support, along with other influences. Employee turnover creates an environment where experienced dispatch personnel are constantly training new employees and working to manage the continuously evolving environment. This dampens moving forward as the "recycle" mode seems to never stop to allow time for proactive planning. Employees end up physically tired, irritable and discouraged.

A permanent fix is difficult. Many different strategies are applied that seek a solution. These include improved hiring practices, background checks (particularly to determine job change frequency), interview process and other steps. Still, the work environment is such that even the best of intentions diminish in the crush of business in a busy dispatch center.

If budgets allow, sending a person to training, that is useful to the individual and the organization, can have positive results. Sending someone to training without talking to them about the supervisor's expectations of attendance, application of new information to the workplace on return, and overall demeanor and engagement, is neglectful.   Perhaps setting up a job-shadowing experience for a day with another dispatch center and getting the employee to see how others conduct business, would add motivation, increase positional understanding and improve position perspective, before the employee "hits the floor running." Change, even for a short period of time that adds value to the work place is an important part of the overall experience.

What Can Be Done

1. Know what each job requires and measure your employee's skills, knowledge, abilities and performance (SKAP's) to the tasks at hand.

2. Talk with employees to determine if they are experiencing problems. Work to fix them if they are present.

3. Remain current with best practices of similar jobs so you know where change may be required. If you deem change is needed, talk with the employees to explore in more detail and then proceed to gather support to take it to the next level.

4. Talk with others in similar positions to learn what they do, how it is done, what their position/work outcome results are, and tips to bring similar changes to your group.

5. Look ahead to potential improvements and changes and align your employees to those future needs so that when the time comes, they can move into position.

6. Keep your own skills current as a supervisor. You, need to be leading from the front, not dropping behind due to self-neglect.

Write your example.

Questions to consider.

1. What steps do you take to keep employees from becoming complacent and with occasional loss of motivation?

2. What techniques do you use to keep employee skills and knowledge at high levels and maximize their motivation and performance?

3. As a supervisor, do you assist employees prepare for promotion and advancement?

18. Leaders evaluate and provide meaningful performance appraisal.

The annual evaluation may be one of the less useful of activities and generally does little except to fulfill some organizational requirement. Few are informative, most are rote statements and little can be gained from receiving one. Not a true statement in all situations, thankfully. A template is filled out and the employee may or may not be able to respond to what was said and offer his or her side of the story. Many of the observations are recent and if performance has been good, it is so reflected. If an issue was of recent vintage, that, too, may be stated but have a negative outcome. And, many employees, generally, are very serious about the evaluation for a number of reasons.

Evaluation should be an ongoing process by the supervisor. Not to find fault but to continually mover the employee forward in his or her job performance.

However, this is completely reversible and the evaluation can be of substantial value, if done right.

From a practical perspective, evaluation should be an on-going activity by the supervisor. Retaining notes allows both immediate and time distant referral to help individuals when needed, to provide accurate information, and to allow being a supervisor from an informed perspective and not based on single events or emotions generated from the moment or those single events.

Both supervisor and employee acknowledge strengths of the employee as a motivator to set positive, growth goals. The supervisor should focus on motivating employees to use their identified strengths to help themselves and others improve.

Helping to move a person forward to utilize their strengths and talents helps you as a supervisor to achieve broader based goals and simultaneously helps the employee to recognize their skills and achievement. This collectively works to improve employees and that of the department/unit. Subsequently, it will also expand upon the employee's knowledge of unit or departmental needs that they might fulfill.

Achievement + Confidence + Motivation = Success

Employees should be actively engaged in their evaluation review, as well. This means asking them to list strengths and weaknesses, to indicate where they would like to improve and asking them for suggestions on how they plan to get there. What can the supervisor and the organization do to assist them in achieving their goals. When most of the input is from the supervisor to the employee and no buy-in is requested, many shrug and continue as before.

If a problem is addressed, ask the employee to provide his or her response and then to analyze what could have been done differently. Follow-up with questions to solicit from the employee their suggestion to fix the problem. That will include being specific and providing a timeline for completion. Once agreement is reached between the supervisor and employee, the effort to bring about change is easier. Specific dates and times should be stated for follow-up meetings. Both the supervisor and employee submit agenda items for that meeting to allow preparation by both. Proof of accomplishments toward change should be recorded and a record kept for future reference. Give praise when due!

The annual evaluation is greatly improved when it reflects personal information that is relevant and accurate to the employee. This is further strengthened when the information covers the entire period (usually a year) and is extracted from a document where the information was recorded. Guess work or insufficient evidence is wrong, if one is to base a twelve-month assessment on for it, as it does little beyond providing rhetoric.

An evaluation that does not value the employee and his or her growth in the organization is of little use.

Supervisors must rise above personality and address performance.

EXAMPLE:

Conducting a leadership class at a State Prison, the discussion by two participants, who shared the same supervisor, stated that their annual evaluations were mirror images, with their names only being changed within the printed report. The supervisor had either prepared or taken an older evaluation and simply changed the name, adding no personal observations or shared reports on the individual's performance. It was considered a "joke" by participants as it contained nothing of value. The attitude toward the supervisor was negative and defensive.

We turned the discussion to what would have been of value to them (from the evaluation/supervisor). The most important information shared was that they wanted an informative, unbiased, personally focused evaluation. They wanted to be able to discuss areas of strength to see where it could help them and they wanted to explore weak areas to find solutions toward improvement.

What Can Be Done

1. The evaluator must keep records or a log on each of his or her subordinates. Maintain a record of information that will aid in writing a meaningful evaluation. One cannot remember with certainty what took place twelve months ago and the last three months are usually what the evaluation is based on.

2. Supervisors should not wait twelve months before having a conversation with an employee, especially when there are issues or problems that require fixing.

3. Addressing issues should take place when they occur, or in close proximity, for time is the enemy. Obtain full facts, schedule a time to meet, tell the employee the purpose of the meeting and hold it.

4. Review the issue or complaint and ask for the employee's input. There are always two sides to every event.

5. Solutions: Ask what the employee will do to make changes and schedule a meeting to establish forward movement steps. This meeting should be within a two to three day window. Add your comments to the plan as supervisor and reach accord on what will be done, how the changes will be measured, and establish a timetable for changes to occur. It is also critical to keep careful notes and insure that change is happening and that it will be sustainable. Appropriate change should take place in the time established. If it has not, then a meeting with the employee is in order. The next step is a corrective action plan, according to the organization's human resource guidelines. Change is not optional, it is all about supervisor and employee resolving the issues and getting the individual back on track with his or her performance.

6. Notes will insure that responsible reporting takes place and those agreements are honored.

The bottom line, the employee is a valued member of the organization and haphazard evaluations send a terrible message, one that clearly states that "you are not valued". We often spend more time focused outward and ignore the individual to whom you have an obligation to guide, coach, mentor and support.

Write your example.

```



```

Questions to consider.

1. Is your evaluation of an employee an end of year pontification about what they have done and any problems encountered? What do you do?

2. What techniques do you use to motivate employees?

3. Are employees actively engaged in guiding their careers? If so, how.

4. What specific techniques do you use that are helpful in employee growth within the organization?

19. Leaders help employees understand the organization's mission and goals and guide them in the delivery of services.

An organization is represented by its employees, for they provide the energy to get the job done, to represent what it stands for and the services or products provided. If employees are doing as they should, profit, effectiveness and efficiency should be the order of the day, thus assisting the organization to achieve its mission and objectives.

Insure that employees know the mission, vision, values and goals. They must be able to articulate them and state how their job fits with each of them. Knowledge diminishes straying from expectations.

With each job there are performance expectations, job task definitions and other contributing influences that indicate the level of job achievement. It is difficult for the employee to self-assess his or her job or to determine if they are specifically meeting the organization's mission, goals, and objectives. We depend on supervisors to provide that level of assessment.

Failing to keep employees informed of their work performance allows them to find comfort using their own personal measures. More often than not, personal measures are also reflective of preference, meaning that what one likes to do is what one does. In an occupation like policing, the options for preference are great as supervision is not constantly present, but more opportunistic and infrequent. There is a large degree of discretion not only in decisions on what the outcome of an encounter will be, but in choice of attention to what one will do when not assigned.

I believe that each employee must be fully aware of what the mission, vision, values and goals are and how they apply to the job they do. If we do not take time to insure this is the state of being with each employee, then we cannot be critical when alteration of performance takes place. Decisions, performance and focus of attention should be on the organization. Apathy often emerges from a lack of understanding; a disengaged employee costs the organization in terms of money and productivity.

It is the duty of every supervisor and administrator to be personally familiar with each of their supervisees and to make sure those who report to them are as fully aware of the organization's mission and goals. It is more difficult to stray from an organization's stated values if they are understood and if the employee is aware that they are being held accountable.

Policy, job descriptions, training, decisions, performance reviews and other actions should be in compliance to mission and goals and not offer a contradictory approach, for that is difficult to reconcile. Meetings, training and individual discussion can help employees understand mission and goals and to answer any questions that arise if clarity and/or conflict exists. It is worth the time and effort on the part of the supervisor in order to guarantee employee alignment.

EXAMPLE:

Samantha had infrequent contact with a supervisor and went about her job without feedback or guidance by others. Awareness of the work environment and the tasks involved soon were categorized as to importance and preference. The more disagreeable of tasks were avoided and additional emphasis placed on other areas. While it did not cause extreme harm, it nonetheless did not fulfill all of the aspects of the job, the organization felt were important. Supervisor review would identify the deficit areas and aim to develop a work plan or discussion on what should be done to address them is perhaps the easiest way to solve the issue.

> Review of employee performance, pointing out strengths and areas of improvement, is a critical function.
>
> The goal is to help the employee develop a work ethic and behavior that is beneficial to everyone in the organization and without.

What Can Be Done?

1. Post, explain and answer questions about the organization's mission and goals. There is no substitute for understanding and the ability to reconcile them with one's job and responsibilities.

2. Engage in discussion with employees using applicable scenarios and ask for their input to fit with mission and goals.

3. Review policy and job descriptions against mission and goals to identify where disconnect exists. Engage with employees as to how reconciliation can take place.

4. Periodically hold group meetings to discuss mission and goals to improve understanding and identify where issues exist. Most issues can be fixed and improved on with broad input.

5. Change occurs whether we want it to or not. It is important to be reflective, aware and scan the environment to learn where change is needed, and adjust accordingly. This may also require revision of mission and goals from time to time. This is not a negative, as keeping current is important to the organization and its employees.

Write your example.

Questions to consider.

1. What is the process you use to identify employee deficits? How are they corrected/

2. What is your protocol for engaging with employees to discuss performance, training, decision-making, and other engagement strategies?

3. Do you hold regular meetings with employees under your direction and are they worth the time?

4. What could you do to improve working conditions and relationships within your section?

20. Leaders Communicate Openly with People.

Many of the employee problems we eventually deal with are the result of a breakdown in communications by the supervisor with the employee. We often wait before we engage in the hope that change will happen and people will comply with wishes or job demands. When time passes and little has changed, individual habit and expectation take hold and make any future alteration very difficult. It is important to maintain contact and communicate with our employees frequently as it reduces rumor and diminishes frustration.

There are some proven techniques that, while simple in concept are powerful in outcome, if applied appropriately. A good leader at any level of the organization must be open and honest with his or her employees. Our daily lives are filled with all manner of activity that engages the mind; and cutting through the clutter is difficult. A leader must clearly portray his or her ideas and thoughts, ask if the other person understands, and explore where differences or misunderstanding exist. Listening is as important as speaking. When one speaks all the time, listening with any sincerity and focus is difficult.

Paraphrasing from others, communications within organizations is difficult given the multiplicity of ideas and thoughts that exist and in how people view themselves and the work they do. There are some important milestones that help determine if the message is being received as intended. They include:

1. People must deal with one another openly and honestly, in other words, increase and maintain the level of trust in each other. If that is not present, there cannot be a sufficient level of meaningful exchange. It has nothing to do with like or dislike, being friends or other influence. It is about the job and the people are the focus and honesty critical.

2. All parties must be responsible to themselves and to others. When deception is viewed or suspected, communications will break down and the consequence is dysfunction and lack of progress.

3. Understand the organization's mission, vision, values and goals and act within their precepts. It is not about you as an individual, but you as part of the organization, its people, products and services. You are an employee first. This will lead to honest discussion within an acceptable framework and not a personal agenda.

4. Create an environment where people feel safe in expressing their views without fear of reprisals. Parameters must be in place, as we do not want insults, personal attacks or unrelated rhetoric interjected that accomplishes little or undermines personal security and mutual respect.

5. Establish an environment where people feel they have a role and are valued as an employee. This should extend to their being willing to contribute and to know they are being heard. An organization primarily consists of the people who work there. Employees should feel that they are the most important asset that the company has. If working collaboratively and with good intent has value, it will enhance the overall organization in positive ways.

6. Decisions emerge from broad input, especially where many people are affected. For that to happen there must be a willingness to listen and value input from employees.

Six Key Concepts

1. Listening is a Key Trait.

If you are preoccupied and half-listening to what is being said or observed, you cannot engage with any depth of genuineness. Your effectiveness will be diminished and the consequence of that will be opportunity lost. Pay attention, give focus, maintain eye contact, and ask for clarification if needed. Body language is important and also conveys a message. Manage your facial and body gestures, maintaining a controlled, approachable and open stance, with your body aligned with your employee, sitting at the same level, facing them as directly as possible.

Supervisors must be aware of several obstructions to listening; many of them are germane to the leader.

- Do not talk more than the individual you want to listen to. You cannot listen intently if you are talking and thinking about what you want to say next.
- Focus on the speaker: listen, look at him or her, and pay attention.
- Let the employee know that you may be making brief notes while they are talking, of points of interest, concern or later questions.
- Keep the discussion focused by not allowing straying to other matters prematurely or for the focus of the meeting/discussion to go "off topic." There is nothing more

How we see ourselves within the organization is of critical importance.

97

frustrating to any employee than to not be heard and/or to feel that the meeting was "useless" or nonproductive.

- Allow people to talk, do not interrupt (unless they are going off-topic). If you have questions, make a brief note so that you can ask them later. Do not interrupt them to ask your questions
- Summarize when the discussion seems to be over, mentioning key points and important aspects. Ask if you have it right.

2. Know the issues and people who are involved.

If you are disengaged, spread too thin, or are distracted by other matters and are there in presence only, you are ineffective. As a supervisor you must be present, engaged and knowledgeable of work process, both pro and con, and to understand where issues exist and what they are.

Supervisors are often distracted with additional work placed on their desk that distracts them from a more direct involvement with employees under their charge. Time becomes a valued commodity and lack of it can have a negative impact on employees whose expectations of the supervisor are diminished.

Plan to be out of the office, away from behind the desk and out among the employees. Talk with them, listen and engage to better know what their concerns and issue are.   Make a list and work to resolve them, if possible. When a 'fix" is not possible, explain that and the reasons why. The key is, "stay involved," a key mantra that will serve you well.

3. Encourage open communications and maintain respectability.

Blowing in at inopportune moments, spending too little time and then exiting is not the model being proposed. You must respect all people who work for you, realize that they are people with ideas, needs, and interests. Respect leads to a willingness to listen to them, take their ideas seriously, and be willing to explore in more detail where the organization might benefit.

Doing this will encourage employees to feel comfortable and to approach you with their thoughts. While you represent the organization as a supervisor you also have responsibility for those who report to you and whom you supervise. Is it a delicate balance, yes it is!

4. Weigh discussions with employees with the organization's mission and goals in mind.

As I have stated time and again, employee work and organization mission and goals must be aligned. . If they are not, the degree of separation runs along a continuum that may unseat balance that is needed for effectiveness and efficiency. Supervisors must discuss with employees the organization's mission and goals as part of the normal discourse, and employees must be aware that their work is expected to align and comply with them.

Discussions about mission and goals seldom take place and in some organizations-- never being the operative word. Missing those aspects allows the employee to make decisions based on preference or choice and this should not be allowed. If a good idea is forthcoming and it has benefit and fits within the organization's mission and goals, the supervisor is encouraged to support it and pass it along to the larger organization.

5. In today's world of multiple communications technology, insure the message is received.

We listen, ask questions and provide feedback to insure we are clear and understand the message. In this manner we help the original communicator know the message was received and is understood. If we do not take that step, and ambiguity or confusion exists, we might not know, potentially sending the receiver off on a different track. One danger is too many methods of communicating that may include e-mail, Facebook, texting, cell phone, agency systems, etc. Be specific and consistent and things do not get lost in application.

Feedback

Carl Rogers provided five categories of feedback that are of value[12]. They are listed in the order in which they most frequently occur in daily communications.

A. Evaluative: Making a judgment about the worth, goodness, or appropriateness of the other person's statement.

B. Interpretive: Paraphrasing — attempting to explain what the other person's statement means.

C. Supportive: Attempting to assist or bolster the other communicator.

D. Probing: Attempting to gain additional information, continue the

---

[12] http://changingminds.org/techniques/conversation/reflecting/rogers_feedback.htm

discussion, or clarify a point.

E. Understanding: Attempting to discover completely what the other communicator means by her statements.

We often do not take the time to insure that both parties in a communication understand the other and that the messages are understood, clear and acceptable, but we need to do that.

6. Breakdown barriers to communications.

Exchange of information or communications is fraught with elements that can lead to misunderstanding. Meanings change between two people as each individual has a mental picture, conceptual understanding, definitions and other personal facets of some subject that are difficult in an exchange with others.

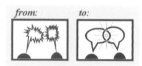

Source: Openstax cnx (cnx.org)

We come from different educational and cultural backgrounds; have different prejudices, bias, perceptions, organizational perspectives and the like. All of these can warp a message, as there is that potentially unknown or unseen set of differences that are present before any exchange takes place. As a result, there is a strong potential for meaning to be lost. Words spoken go through a variety of filters particular to the individual speaking (as specified in the list of differences, herein), as a result possibly removing critical content and/or meaning. We must be aware of the barriers and take action to insure we have overcome them in a way that results in complete exchange of information, in other words, a completed loop of communication from sender to receiver.

One way to insure the message has been received is to ask the individual to repeat back what they heard. At that time one can insure that what one thinks they have heard is indeed what the sender intended, clarify any points of miscommunication that might be identified in the "feedback" loop. Does it take time? Yes, it does! Is it worth the time? Yes, for returning to a subject more than once requires additional time that is not necessary if the initial communication was clearly received and understood as to initial message and intent.

EXAMPLE:

This is an example of a department-wide communications exchange. There is value in this approach as well. The Tallahassee, FL, Police Department held monthly "vertical staff meetings" where representatives of all sections and units of the department were represented. No uniforms and no high ranking officers, except for the Chief of Police. The intent was to allow lower ranking members of both the sworn officer and civilian employees to have a say, to be heard, and to expect that the issue or problem would be addressed. Communication was two-ways, and a response to the problem would be given as soon as information was available or at the next meeting. Not all issues could be resolved during the meeting. The key was the open discussion that took place allowing individuals would be heard. Solutions would be sought to correct issues that were troubling.

What Can Be Done

1. Be fully present and attentive to your employees. They are your prime responsibility.

2. Listen. Genuinely listen. Show interest, ask questions to clarify that what you heard is accurate and show that you have a clear understanding of the intent of their message. To be other than this will result in you losing valuable respect and trust from your supervisees.

4. Be aware there are many barriers to clear communications. Know the person you are meeting with (i.e., cultural, religious or life experiences that might impact their way of communicating or relating to the organization, their job, or you! Do what you can to overcome any barriers so that there is a clear road to full communication between you and them.

5. Never assume your message was received and understood. Ask questions that seek to insure the information exchanged is clear.

6. Work within the organizations mission, vision, values and goals. All else creates division of purpose.

Write your example.

Questions to consider.

1. What are the parameters or judgment decision points that you use to create an open and honest environment with your subordinates?

2. What is your organization's policy on establishing and maintaining a collaborative working environment?

3. In your experience, what are the major barriers to open communications? How did you overcome them?

4. What are the barriers that you have encountered from employees that dampen communications and ferment complaint?

21. Leaders insist on resilient ethical and moral behavior.

A leader must clearly define and explain the organization's ethics and morality expectations as a foundational base to performance and behavior. A challenge, almost unattainable and certainly not a "quick" goal, but one that will take consistent and clear effort that is engaging and inclusive of all stakeholders.

How is this to be done? Leaders must exemplify organizational ethics serving as an example to others. The leader's behavior and that of their employees must be compatible with the expectations and demands of the organization. The goals and underlying philosophies of the organization are explored and the probabilities for employee compliance should be discussed and examined in the light of day. Where identified differences exist, they must be clarified and appropriate resolution determined.   Employees, whose actions are contrary to what the organization expects, both ethically and morally, will require specific action plans to bring them into alignment. The organization hires people to make them successful in the delivery of service or product. When this expectation is not met, immediate action must be taken to correct the situation.

Lisa Stewart, 2006, in her article "Developing Ethical Leadership,[13]" provided ten characteristics of ethical leadership. You are directed to the article for more detail. Note that bullet comments are added by this author.

1. Articulate and embody the purpose and values of the organization.

   - How do employees do this? It is part of their training, ongoing evaluation, focus discussion by supervisors and examination of work performance to see that compliance is in fact in place?
   - If not, it should be?

2. Focus on organizational success rather than personal ego.

   - The opposite condition is that unsuccessful organizations do not long remain in existence. Working to make the organization succeed also makes the individual successful.

3. Find the best people and develop them.

---

[13]. Stewart, L. (2006). Developing Ethical Leadership. Business Roundtable Institute for Corporate Ethics. www.corporate-ethics.org

- Selection of quality employees is a critical responsibility of any organization. We are generally a collection of people who represent the organization and if they are high quality, dedicated, focused and content, we generally have harmony and success.

4. Create a living conversation about ethics, values and the creation of value for stakeholders.

- If, the organization tells new employees about its ethics and values expectations, explains what they are and mean, but never follow-up to insure they are applied, we should not expect that adherence or even occasional thoughts about them to take place.
- If you expect employees to comply, you must have occasional discussion, comparison of expectation to practice, and determine ways to remain focused, from the newest employee to the CEO.

5. Create mechanisms of dissent.

- Pardon the analogy, but back room bitching is about as valuable as an empty gas tank. Complaining is normal, sometimes healthy, and may provide a pathway to positive change.
- Uncontrolled complaining, routine and with vehemence, is destructive.
- Administration and supervisors must create opportunities to address concerns, issues and problems. This can be scheduled meetings, individual discussion, inquiry and other mechanisms that may naturally exist in the organization.
- The key, do not let issues fester or they may get out of hand. Most of the issues are fixable and if known early, preventable.

6. Take a charitable understanding of others' values.

- Hard and fast adherence to rules and policy will achieve compliance, but they also effectively diminish innovation and motivation.
- One's life is not totally centered in work for most people. We also know that there are many influences in life that affect one's employment. Realizing that, we should be attentive to needs and issues, that while not work based, do impact in multiple ways.
- Effective supervisors engage with employees and to assist them overcome issues that inhibit work productivity. Yes, it is a fine line at times, but when the employee opens the door, do not let it shut in his or her face, engage with them.

7. Make tough calls while being imaginative.

- As have others, I received a few "chewing out" sessions by a supervisor and the experience was not pleasant. Those that were of most value included a "What can <u>we</u> do to fix the issue?" Both the employee and the supervisor forming a partnership to make positive change.

- We can insist on change, mandate it and evaluate if it occurs. Often times there is residual anger, mistrust and other feelings, as only a partial "fix" took place.
- Importantly, the supervisor should endeavor to work with the individual to insure successful outcomes. It requires a commitment to engage with the employee and devote sufficient time with them to achieve desired change.

8. Know the limits of the values and ethical principles they live.

> **Providing leadership, coaching, understanding, time and effort requires additional supervisor energy. But, at the end of the day, it may well be the one of the most fulfilling of duties.**

- Expectations can be over the top and that too is not healthy. I suggest some people might have slightly different values and ethics, not way out of bounds, but to the left or right and still be an effective employee.
- The challenge is when these differences are too far apart, it is difficult to reconcile.

9. Frame actions in ethical terms.

- Once we stray from ethical decisions and resulting behavior, we enter that gray area of question and occasional confusion.
- Clear and unambiguous statements of purpose, and behind actions taken, establish a line where expectations are well-defined. Weakening the decision and accommodating deviation from the organization's expectation, opens the door to the proverbial Pandora's Box[14].

10. Connect the basic value proposition to stakeholder support and societal legitimacy.

- Take police as the example. When police service deviates from public expectation, we have the potential for disagreement. Certainly, police officer performance and behavior is based on education, training, law and policy.
- The public is not privy to that level of knowledge and may not understand why some actions are taken and in the manner executed.

---

[14] . Today the phrase "to open Pandora's box" means to perform an action that may seem small or innocent, but that turns out to have severely detrimental and far-reaching consequences. Source: http://en.wikipedia.org/wiki/Pandora%27s_box

- The distance between police action and public interpretation is generally minor, but occasionally a case occurs where major division takes place. The incident itself will be examined and some outcome achieved. I speak to the common ground of understanding that says the action/s taken by the police were ethical and their purpose grounded in sound principal and consistency.
- Therefore, police and public must spend some time in examining procedure and purpose and how it all reconciles between the parties.
- It must be legal, represent sound practice, reflect society's expectation, and achieve a level of understanding between the public and the police.

The point is, we try to define and apply generalized terms to more specific expectations and it is not easily accomplished. It is about how we live, what we value, what we are willing to do and not do within policy and rules. Conflict arises and we find we are not in compliance with one or many aspects of the organization's expectations. That realization necessitates shifting our thoughts and corresponding behavior to make a correction.

Definitions to Understanding.

For purposes of this material, the following definitions are offered. What has been added are other considerations that weigh in on ethics and moral considerations, for they are integral and impact the eventual outcomes of our decisions.

Ethics: Rules or standards governing the conduct of a person or of members of a profession (Examples are codes of ethics, mission and values statement, etc.). The study of how our decisions affect other people.

Examples

- Responding to the homeless situation, Ben & Jerry's opened a store in Harlem, NY, and employed homeless people to serve ice cream.

- Paul Newman earmarks all of the profits from *Newman's Own* food products for various charities, such as the Hole in the Wall Gang, a camp for children with terminal cancer.

Dilemma: A situation requiring a choice between two options that are, or seem to be, equal, unfavorable or mutually exclusive. Having to make a decision where the answer is not clear and the choices are more than one. Taking a course of action that has multiple outcome possibilities, but where delay is unwarranted and action must be taken.

- Current law requires mandatory arrest by a police officer of a person suspected of violence in a domestic violence case. That mandatory outcome may not be the desired course of action, were it not mandatory.

Ethical Dilemma: A situation where the rules of right conduct appear violated regardless of the action taken; alternative actions are mutually exclusive. Weighing out all aspects the choice you make will adversely affect someone, yet the situation cannot be left unattended.

- A Social Services case worker is aware that a single woman is working nights to support herself and two children, ages ten and five. The ten year old is left in charge of the younger child at night, while the mother is at work. State policy prohibits this situation. If the case worker brings charges, it will create an even worse situation, disrupt the family, bring additional expense to the State and may not achieve an outcome that is desirable.

Integrity: Strict adherence to a standard of value or conduct. Personal honesty.

- All people experience temptation at some point in time. It can range from minor to substantial, meaning that if engaged in, the outcome is wrong on its face.
- The decision process to proceed or not is often measured in minutes and what is ultimately done, may subsequently lead to greater issue.
- Asking oneself if what is proposed is right and listening to the response of conscience, should dictate action taken.

Bias: A preference or inclination, especially one that inhibits impartial judgment. These can include racial, ethnic, religious, gender, handicap, sexual preference, and age biases.

- Close examination often discloses that we all harbor bias of something. The resulting feelings and opinion may well pose a challenge to one's demeanor and resulting actions.
- How we act, based on the judgments we make, are the defining measures of our ability to manage bias.

Prejudice: Adverse judgment or opinion formed beforehand or without knowledge or examination of the facts.

- Seeing someone or something that evokes a reaction. It may be based on race, gender, employment, attitude, hair style, expression, activity, or any number of triggers where one's emotions and feelings are illuminated.

Stereotyping: Categorizing the qualities of a person based on popular generalizations about the group to which that person belongs. An oversimplified conception, opinion, or images of a group of people are among ways we stereotype.

- While society is changing, mellowing out from earlier beliefs and standards, we have not yet removed all causes to reaction at something seen, heard, smelled, touched or aware of. Issues of sexual preference, same sex marriage, use of drugs, religious belief, and of a variety of behaviors that bring an emotional response can be questioned.
- Why the need to trash someone or some group? Where does this emerge from and why is it present? When recognized, what can and should we do about it.

We must be resilient in our determination to maintain behavior and actions that are morally right and ethically strong, resisting any and all diversion.

EXAMPLE:

Wendy was aware that Julia needed extra money to address a family issue. If left unaddressed, it would potentially result in a heartbreaking outcome, one that would have lasting negative impact on Julia.

Wendy became aware that Julia had inadvertently discovered a way to obtain nearly $1,000 from work specific funds. In violation of company policy, she took the money. The money resolved the crisis that she and her family were facing.   Wendy knew that the source of the money was not harmed in this action and that both parties were in agreement, yet, company policy prohibited that type of action.

The questions we must ask ourselves are:

1. Should Wendy report Julia to her supervisor?

2. Should Wendy say anything to Julia?

3. Should Wendy demand that Julia give the money back?

4. Should Wendy mind her business and say nothing.

5. Are there other possible actions that Wendy could or should take?

What Can Be Done

1. Be comfortable with how you define morality and ethical behavior. Ambiguity is the enemy and if too many exceptions are part of the discussion, it is difficult to hold anyone to any level of accountability, except for the very worst of behaviors.

2. Clearly define and tell your employees how you feel, how you identify appropriate behavior, what is not correct and will be addressed (and how), and what the organization expects.

3. Live the example. Your behavior and actions will be the best example for what is expected by those others who work for the organization and report to you.

4. Address violations as they occur. Delay in repairing any damaging behavior will only serve to make the situation worse.

5. Have discussions with employees about morality and ethical behavior as it pertains to their work.

6. Ask yourself what barriers exist and how they can be overcome? What are the dilemmas that employees encounter and how are they handled? How should they be handled? Identify and clarify the problem and then immediately address the need.

Write your example.

Questions to consider.

1. How do you clearly define and explain change, policy, things to watch out for, etc.?

2. How do you engage with an employee whose behavior is not following policy?

3. When an employee is stating something that seems of a biased nature, what do you do?

4. Conflict occasionally arises within an organization. As a supervisor how do you handle it, if it occurs?

22. Leaders personally adhere to a strong code of conduct and demand it of others in the organization.

We seldom hear about an employee "code of conduct," as more emphasis is placed on rules, policy, procedure and expectations. A lot of assumption is made about conduct, when in fact it must be discussed and explored in sufficient depth to connect all employees with its principles and practices.

A code of conduct consists of a set of rules that clearly state the accepted practices and responsibilities of individual employees by the organization. In practice, the depth of indoctrination and adherence varies, as one would expect. And, a code of conduct is stronger when employees have the opportunity to weigh in with their thoughts and recommendations, before implementation. In some of the more public organizations, such as police departments, we are more likely to find an inclusive policy and adherence rules. But, even there, diversity and lack of motivation effort can diminish outcomes.

The values, principles, and rules pertaining to behavior, standards and other important guidelines to decision-making and performance, are often left to generalities and individual interpretation, which is often not sufficient. When something negative occurs, the organization's policy is brought forth and the formal approach of discipline quickly becomes the guiding principle or response.

A solid code of conduct should be clearly defined and adopted by organizations. Every employee, from the CEO to the newest hire, should be expected to learn them, and each person provided the opportunity to discuss their intent and how they apply to the work being done. Internal behaviors and external appearances are manifest in performance. Clearly answering the question as to what is acceptable and what is not, is the basic foundation for defining the code.

Wasted time through lack of proper behavior, conflict and resolution efforts, and in some instances legal action, emerges from actions that do not reflect the conduct demanded by the organization. To minimize problems, a code of conduct must be realistic, appropriate to the organization and its' services and expected employee behavior. A code of conduct applies to all members of the organization and exceptions should not be allowed. The goal is to seek compliance, protect employee and employer rights, be legal and ethical, and establish a respect for self and others in adhering to the underlying responsibilities that it implies.

Leadership staff must be aware of and protect the rights of the employees as well as the organization. This symbiotic relationship is critical if success for all is the goal. There are many barriers, self-imposed and lingering through tradition, that can pose harmful obstacles. They need to be identified, abolished and replaced with a new spirit that seeks commonality of purpose, clear understanding of expectations, behavior and performance appropriate for effective work productivity and rewards.

A code of conduct is unique to the requirements of the organization and the needs of all and it must be carefully crafted to illustrate the right values and interests. This is a task that requires work and attentive effort. A code of conduct is not a generic document and it varies by the specific professions, organizations and includes individuals who shape their own work performance.

The website of <u>Life Skills Coaches Association of British Columbia</u>[15] provides six reasons why an organization should have a code of conduct. They include:

- to define accepted/acceptable behaviors;
- to promote high standards of practice;
- to provide a benchmark for members to use for self-evaluation;
- to establish a framework for professional behavior and responsibilities;
- as a vehicle for occupational identity;
- As a mark of occupational maturity.

So, while seemingly complex, upon completion, the code of conduct document provides a clear set of standards that should be understood by all employees. It will guide action, behavior, and performance while establishing parameters around the often conflicting expectations and performance issues.

<u>EXAMPLE</u>:

Brenda was a compassionate and employee centered supervisor. Most of her crew respected that attitude and worked with her, acknowledging that on occasion she seemed more on the soft side by not addressing problems that a particular employee, Sidney, seemed to constantly bring to the table, either in person or through bad behavior that others complained about.

The latest incident upset nearly seventy-five percent of the employees, yet none were willing to cause Brenda additional work, for it seemed she was particularly loaded with deadline tasks at the moment. So, the employees were generally angry and complaining among themselves about Sidney's

---

[15] http://www.calsca.com/

aberrant behavior. During a work break, a minor skirmish broke out when the offending employee bragged about his escapades and the fact that the supervisor was a "weak leader" and was not about to do anything about it. George, affectionately called "hammer," suddenly grabbed Sidney and told him to "shut up, stop being a jerk and get back to work!"

Shaken by the incident, Sidney filed a complaint against George for assault and intimidation at the workplace. Brenda found the complaint on her desk and, after reading it, set out to investigate. As details of the incident were collected, Brenda became aware of the previous bad behaviors of Sidney, the details of which she was not intimately aware of.

If you were to advise Brenda on this incident, what would your advice include? What role would the organization's code of conduct play, and why?

<u>What Can Be Done</u>

1. Every organization needs a well written, clear and comprehensive code of conduct to guide employee behavior and actions.

2. A code of conduct must be symbiotic with the organization's policy, procedures, rules and other guiding documents.

3. A developing code of conduct must have input across the organization by employees at all roles and duties to truly represent the best practices and culture. They must, of course, be honorable, and not just a "free will" document.

4. A code of conduct is about proper attitude and behavior and looks at performance, offering acceptable and preferred employee actions. It is a values statement that people are charged with adhering to.

If your organization does not have an approved code of conduct, it should be seriously considered. Behavior utilizing accepted standards will help reduce individualism which is deemed inappropriate.

Write your example.

Questions to Consider.

1. Does your agency have a code of conduct?

2. What are the positive and negative sides of this issue?

3. When employee conduct is questioned, what is the process to address it?

4. As a supervisor, would you prefer to have the responsibility to manage conduct issues, or should that be deferred to higher authority?

23. Leaders make sound decisions based on the acquisition of full information and careful analysis.

Millions of decisions are made daily and most of them have little to no impact on the planet or the people who inhabit it. Individually we engage in decision-making across broad categories, such as what time to get up, what to wear, what is on my "to do" list, what meetings do I have, how do I approach items A and B, etc. Many decisions only impact on the individual but many include others to varying degrees of importance.

Decision-making ability is not automatic, it is learned behavior. It is something we develop, learn from our mistakes and improve on over time. Not all decisions require the same response or depth of inquiry and the final outcomes also vary in depth of rightness.

Leadership and decision-making are symbiotic, meaning they go hand in hand with one's responsibility, position, role and function in an organization. No decision, large or small, should be taken for granted. A single bad decision can have catastrophic outcomes, if the event or circumstance is critical to final outcomes. People above and below your position judge you on your decision-making.

Sorting Out Information

The ability to make a decision is dependent on available information, knowledge, and awareness of the situation, expectations, policy dictates, the people involved and numerous other variables. Sound decisions emerge from being able to process and sort information, arriving at a solution based on informed reasoning. You need accurate and a depth of information, to ask questions, inquire of others, and determine what has worked successfully in other similar situations. Not all decisions require this depth of inquiry, but many do, and thoroughness is critical in that process.

Certainly not every decision requires that depth of process, but important and far reaching outcomes do mandate care in what you do. Skill in filtering out unnecessary information and using critical data as the basis for your decision is also a learned skill and one that is important to all leaders.

How we get full information before decisions are rendered.

Often a story is told or someone drops a dime on an event they want to point out, but without being implicated; a motivation from many points of perspective. And just as often we react, an emotional response, and often short sighted and way to hollow to the facts once they are known. Being able to manage one's response until all the facts are known is the only correct action or response. How often have we heard something or partially observed an action without fully understanding the whole story, but in our haste to respond, do so without full information. When new facts emerge they may well change the outcome and sometimes it is more difficult to fix the supervisor's mistake than what the offending employee was alleged to have done. Point being, we should never move with haste when full information has not been obtained and verified.

Gathering and Using Information

Where is the information you need to make the decision? If it lies with other people, ask them. If they are concerned about personal jeopardy or harm, determine how they can be protected within policy and procedure. If it involves a database, go to someone who is most familiar and ask them to provide that information to you. If it needs explanation, obtain it and do not try to fathom it out yourself.

Regardless, drill down until you hit bedrock, for missing information is as harmful to your decision process as no information at all. You cannot make firm and reasonable decisions with half-baked information. Too much missing information leads to incomplete decisions, for you cannot react to what you do not know.

Analysis and Application

All relevant information must be examined, considered against policy determine its applicable value to the task at hand. Once it is clear and understood, it must be applied to the situation being examined. An informed decision is important and when based on fact, it is more likely to be correct than not.

It would be remiss not to mention that all information of relevance and which will be used to make decisions, must be validated as accurate and representing that which you are exploring. Conjecture, rumor, and other forms of soft information should be rejected as unworthy.

Decisions on Outcomes

Personally, I feel it is permissible to inquire of others who might have information, being conscious of their role, peer pressure, knowledge of the situation and other variables that may sway their comments. This is not an automatic step for personnel and/or Union rules may prohibit some action in specific circumstances. Engaging the employee, asking for clarification, feedback and explanation can also help clarify and process what the supervisor will eventually do.

Final Decisions

Policy will state the extent to which a supervisor can produce the final decision and what must be passed up the chain of command. When in doubt, consult with someone who is able to officially render an opinion and the capacity to enter into the decision. It is less about CYA and more toward correctness and review to insure that fairness and unbiased decisions emerge.

EXAMPLE:

Rumor reached the supervisor that one of his officers was leaving his patrol area to check on his wife whom he felt was being unfaithful. Asking fellow officers to cover for him had grown thin and they were complaining. Yet, no one came to him directly, but it was surmised that tolerance had grown thin and a solution was needed.

The decision was to ask the officer straight out or to observe his actions and catch him in the act, if true. Considering the officer, the relationship between the two, prior issues and the likelihood of having him truthful led to selecting the observation model. Having a factual example of leaving his assigned patrol area and knowing what was taking place was believed to be a stronger position and one where denial was less apt to happen.

What Can Be Done

1. Do not react to unverified facts. What you hear might not be accurate or certainly contain the full set of details needed to make decisions.

2. Unless critical, take time to gather facts and relevant information. Go to the sources that offer that information, make the request, and insure confidentiality.

3. Analyze the information for understanding and to see if additional needs might be missing.

4. Make decisions on a course of action based on facts, policy and authority granted.

5. Consult with the employee for his or her statements and side of the story.

6. Make a decision on your response, write it down, meet with the employee, discuss and set in place follow-up and reporting due from that employee to you, the frequency and expectations.

7. Inform whomever else you must to insure that policy is being followed.

8. Conduct regular follow-up to insure correction takes place and that it is likely not to reoccur.

Write your example.

Questions to consider.

1. When a decision is made that someone disagrees with, is it reviewed and if a different procedure is needed in the future, that discussion takes place with all parties involved?

2. Does your agency have a program to assist employees in making the right decisions based on the situation and circumstances?

3. With time permitting, are decisions carefully explored to gather relevant information before committing to a direction or process?

24. Leaders encourage innovation and best practices.

Innovation and creativity is not on the mind of most employees who enter the workplace on Monday morning. This is not to say it does not exist, rather other needs and immediate concerns take precedent.

What impacts innovation and creativity within each individual worker? Possible influences could be: the behavior of one's supervisor, the demands of the job, how others that you work with think and behave, general workplace climate and culture, and so on. Innovation and creativity are generally encouraged, recognized and rewarded by those organizations where support is provided, and missing in others where it is not readily recognized.

What do we mean by innovation and creativity and why are they a consideration in most organizations? For our purposes we are not focusing so much on new products or technology. Instead, we are focusing on the effectiveness and efficiency of work improvement, on new ways to accomplish the same job with fewer steps, on being able to do the job with less cost or investment, and on achieving the same or even better results, at less cost.

Agbor[16] (2008) offers sound advice for leader engagement in creativity and innovation. He speaks of the leader being the catalyst and source of organizational creativity by implementing strategies that allow it to happen. Spontaneous innovation may occur, but generally the routine nature of the job becomes prominent, and moving beyond its boundaries is seldom sought.

We work within an environment of job function, worker performance, rules and procedures. When combined with personal likes and dislikes, we often find that the individual "tailors" the rules and requirements and/or performance standards to fit themselves and their comfort level or level of competence. If one is standing at a machine all day long, making minor adjustments to a product, innovation is likely to be at a minimal level. A police officer, however, is able to initiate a number of choices within his/her workday, thereby defining what he or she likes and prefers to engage in when not on a call for service.

---

[16] . Agbor, Emmanuel. (2008). Creativity and Innovation: The Leadership Dynamics. Journal of Strategic Leadership, 1(1), 39-45.

To elicit change and set the stage for creating, motivating and nurturing innovation and creativity, is it critical to engage the individual worker for their input and suggestions. When a company sets a goal for change, through innovation and creativity, it is most likely to occur when the company/leadership works from the individual worker, on up. If each individual feels that they have input into company change, they are much more likely to buy into that process.

Organizational culture also plays a role. If innovation and creativity are not the norm, then employees are probably not focused on them or engaged in thinking about new ideas or new ways to perform their jobs/tasks. In situations like this, any effort toward company changes (as in changing any individual's way of doing their job), will necessitate involvement, commitment and support by leaders and supervisors. Inspiring others is not an automatic gift in being a supervisor. It must be nurtured and encouraged, supported and applied to the organization's needs. In this case, this model for change must start from the top, down, in order to educate and prepare the companies leadership team in how to engage each individual employee in the change process in the most positive and effective manner.

EXAMPLE:

Geographic Information Systems Analysts, a new position in the Charlotte-Mecklenburg Police Department, began with the advent of the agency's conversion from traditional law enforcement to Community Problem Oriented Policing (CPOP). GIS analysis was one of the core transitional pieces to full implementation of CPOP.

It was not long before it was clear that the group of Analysts were exceptional individuals who were forging new ground with each new application, which was work done with field officers and administrators as they addressed long-standing community problems. Popularity of the skills and abilities of this group was soon in huge demand, far out-stripping the time and effort available.

Not discouraging the overwhelming number of requests for assistance was important to the new approach to policing. Therefore, it was imperative that the division (GIS Analysts) be trained to refrain from telling staff that we could not fulfill their needs at that time without risking the potential of the larger organization of staff members losing interest. GIS staff was empowered to make their own decisions, establish timetables, schedules, assignments and general work. There was reluctance by the analysts in saying "no" to any and all requests coming in to their unit, resulting in their accepting more work than they could efficiently and thoroughly handle. In other words, they now became at risk for impacting the quality of their work, which could ultimately impact the future success and reputation of their department.

<u>What Can Be Done</u>

1. Where do the seeds of innovation and creativity lie? Understanding where the potential for positive change can take place is the first step.

2. Who will be affected by new innovation/creativity, and does the extent of potential change warrant the time and energy necessary to implement a change process.

3. Listen to your employees who propose an idea that seeks to effect change. Ask questions and determine the depth of the idea and its fit to the organization. If sound, find ways to support them and more forward.

4. Balance time devoted to new program ideas so as not to put other duties behind schedule.

5. As leader, it is important to insure that employee work in their primary function is maintained, and that blending in new project ideas balances that work.

Write your example.

Questions to consider.

1. As a supervisor, what methods and techniques do you use to inspire your subordinates?

2. Do employees respond well to motivation and inspiration efforts by the supervisor?

3. What is your agency's method of introducing change to employees and to gauge their response?

4. When barriers to change are discovered, how are they overcome?

25. Leaders are aware of the need for self-development and personal growth.

Self-development is often equated to doing something fun for oneself, playing to an interest, hobby or event that brings personal satisfaction in pursuit of self-selected goals. This is not what we refer to here. When we consider an individual's effectiveness, in executing their duties, we must consider the importance of continuing self-development and its application to the work they do.

The structure of the world has evolved to now include an expectation that the individual has responsibility for his or her growth and that it is not just dependent on the organization the person works for. There are multiple opportunities, some free, some with a substantial cost, and others that fall in-between. Separating the employee from his or her leadership ability is a logical dividing line, for being a leader is not dependent on the rank or position you hold. It cannot be, as rank does not speak to skills, knowledge, abilities, attitude, education and training and how those factors are applied to the job.

Of critical importance in the area of self-development is the training of supervisors, for they hold a critical place in directing success within the organization. Maintaining professional proficiency, while encouraged by administration, really falls to the individual him or herself: a truly personal responsibility. If the supervisor feels that he or she will be valued, supported, given self-empowerment to achieve new heights and engage in becoming of greater value to the organization, many or most will do so. In relationship to this critical need is the knowledge that many organizations are not actively tracking employee skill and knowledge needs, as applied to the job, and that void can be costly.

Thus we are faced with both a dilemma and a challenge. The challenge is, how can we motivate the individual to increase his or her skills, to perform at higher levels and to be not only a self-starter but someone who knows what to do when opportunity presents itself? We must reward performance that meets the organizations mission, vision, values and goals and encourage continued growth and development. To do less means we should not anticipate or expect much in the way of change to occur.

The United States Department of Defense has a 15 page document that outlines an individual development planning process. The document provides steps and considerations for growth. The excellent reference document is found at: http://www.usuhs.mil/chr/idp.pdf

Supervisors must also be aware of the needs of those who report to them. Remaining job ready is of value and critical in performing one's duty. It insures that employees have the opportunity to remain viable to the organization for which they work. Supervisors point this out to employees, help them acquire opportunities, and provide genuine interest in outcomes.

A study conducted by this author examined police officer supervisory personnel attending the North Carolina Criminal Justice Academy's management development program. A major outcome of that study was the need for pre-, during and post-training review by the supervisor with the employee who was attending the program. The following illustrates this concept.

Supervisor Role with Employee Training

Pre- Training	During-Training	Post-Training
• Meet with the employee and discuss the pending training to help convey the value for the person and the organization. • Express your interest in the individual being successful in acquiring helpful skills and knowledge. • Provide your support for attending. • Ask them what they want to do with the training when they return. • Ask them if there are barriers to surmount by attending the trainings and work to eliminate them or reduce their impact.	• Prevent the organization from contact or interruption of the employee while at training. • Assign others including you to help keep the duties of the individual attending training from accumulating. • Manage inquiries and handle if possible. • Make frequent contact to inquire if anything is needed.	• Schedule a meeting with the individual on his or her return to work, soon after completion of the training. • Ask them what was learned and what could be delivered to other employees for their benefit also. • Ask them what they want to do with the training. • Accommodate changes in their work if possible and of benefit to all. • Do not let the new skills languish, put them to work and demonstrate their value to the person and the organization.

We are all familiar with attending training and on return; no one asks what was learned that is of value to your job, to the organization and to others with whom you work. It was as if you never left, for no one asks or shows any interest in the outcomes of the training. That seems rather sad and certainly is an inadequate response by the supervisor, let alone the organization

EXAMPLE:

Harold attended the Federal Bureau of Investigation Command Officer School, an eleven week program at the Quantico facility. Assignment is prestigious and the person learns many new skills, acquires new knowledge, generates excellent relationships with other officers from around the world and enjoys renewed motivation.

On completion of this prestigious training and return to duty, a conversation with his supervisor, both before attending and on return, was the value of the experience and how it would be applied to his job responsibilities. He acquired new knowledge, helpful information and practice to apply to his specific work role and the overall organization, but it was not formally utilized. Training others in specific aspects of his new knowledge seemed to be of critical value and would have been appropriate as part of the obligation following return to duty. A contract with his workplace to apply new information should have been part of the authorization to allow attendance.

What Can Be Done

1. Remain current on your job duties and the expertise required to be effective. Know yourself and your skills, knowledge, abilities and required actions to be effective and seek access to upgrade where needed.

2. Conduct mini-needs assessments to insure that you know, factually, what exists, and not depend on conjecture and supposition.

3. Know your employees and address their expectations. If you identify a deficit in what they need to know to do their job, seek training to help them acquire it.

4. Help establish career goals, make a list and what is needed to achieve them and establish a plan to fulfill each step.

6. Identify what is of value, necessary and critical to job performance skills and what will help move employees forward, not just maintain status quo.

Write your example.

Questions to consider.

1. How is individual responsibility encouraged and rewarded by the organization

2. How does the agency reward performance that meets the organizations mission, vision, values and goals?

3. Does your agency do a pre-training discussion with the employee who is going to attend training, to insure that proper understanding is in place about the expected behavior, learning outcomes, and application to his or her job on return?

4. As a supervisor, do you periodically review the skills, knowledge and abilities of your employees to insure they are current and appropriate to the job?

Summary.

Leaders are represented by every shape, size and ilk and most are aware of their role in the organization. Truth be known, leadership may be one of the more elusive responsibilities ever assumed. When two or more people are engaged in some event, task or duty, the potential for challenge remains. This is further complicated with influences of disagreement, limited compliance and other manifestation that either directly or indirectly impact on the outcome. The goal is to fulfill the organization's mission and do so with maximum effectiveness and minimum disruption. Imposing outcomes, versus willing compliance, is a skill not inherent within all of us. The goal is to fulfill mission and to do so with maximum effectiveness and minimum disruption.

If we are seeking a list of required leader skills, knowledge and abilities, to make a definitive list that everyone adopts and leads to success, what are we talking about? Perhaps making leadership a one size fits all model, infused with flexibility, we are better served if we expect it will more resemble the situation we find ourselves engaged in, than some lofty characteristic. Utilizing basic and underlying principles, represented by a series of assumptions, allows an internal process to occur. The leader must be able to observe, gather, process and provide guidance and direction without undue lapse of time.

> The leader must be a student of the situation, to pull together relevant bits of information, process them and arrive at a course of action that results in a successful outcome and reflects the organization's mission and goals. This will reinforce future employee decision-making. Leadership is by example in that we often emulate what we experience.

Using rank or a position of authority as a definition of leadership is fraught with more missteps than walking in the dark, if the truth were known. The position is as hollow or fulfilled as the person who occupies it. Great leaders often carry high rank and position, but the inverse can be said for poor leaders, who may also rise to the top, but occasionally with all manner of accompanying baggage. The challenge is to get it right, the first time out of the gate, and with the expected outcome consistently achieved.

We offer insight to a belief that leadership is not a single bundle of characteristics and talents; rather it incorporates the ability to manipulate the situation and its constituent parts, in a way that achieves success. To explore how this might be possible, it seemed prudent to focus on leader traits and assertions that make sense. If we have a list of situations and corresponding models to address them, could we not, select applications that raise the outcome to greater success?

126

We need to be clear about the roles we perform as they often identify personal motivation and engagement in our work. We cannot overreach the limits of our education, training and experience, nor should we. Achievement or the potential for reaching levels of success is not done with tenacity alone, for we must use the power of others, their needs, motivations, interests and desire to do well, as part of the plan that emerges for any activity that we engage in. Principles apply and utilize tools of the trade, apply common sense and encourage optimism. When they are missing, the search for success is more elusive.

Anchored in leadership is a focus that brings others to a common goal and alignment with the tasks at hand. This is strengthened with cohesive attitudes and a willingness to collaborate utilizing varying levels of fortitude. This leads to successful outcomes and a cohesive group of workers who are centered in the organization's mission, vision, values, and goals.

The twenty-five assertions represent a collection of principles gleaned from others who have held positions of responsibility. They are not intended to be empirically valid, nor are they labeled as the pathway to success. In combination with an individual's skills, knowledge, abilities and experience; situations often result in selecting a course of action that is enhanced with guidance from an available framework. We call them assertions, as their practiced application leads to confirmation of anticipated and expected outcomes.

To be the leader you seek, you must step out of a narrow role, expand to include action by example, teacher, coach, disciplinarian, to support others in their time of need and attain a level of flexibility that permits choice and corresponding action. You must balance people and organization, finding the most effective and efficient path where mission, vision, values and goals are fulfilled and in a manner that also brings forth the best in employees. This demands a depth of strength and commitment, not present in all people.

And finally, a self-test to determine the level of stress you or others might be experiencing, is in the appendix. Why is this important? We know that stress, adversity and trauma impacts of individual behavior. Employees who are experiencing excessive stress will find that it impacts on their work performance and other life engagements. If stress is found to be harmful, steps can be taken to moderate it and help the individual return to personal balance.

The following book, written by this author in collaboration with a colleague, refers to peer coaching, a tool most valued in organizations. It is priced low to encourage wide use in organizations, as employee well-being is of critical value to well-functioning organizations.

A second manuscript, linked to leadership, focuses on the importance of supervision. The book was written to offer insight to practical and applied supervision information. This is a "cut to the chase" book, where the reader can find the appropriate topic of inquiry and determine if and how it serves their need.

Leadership, like most personal functions, emerges from the person. We offer this information to assist you to determine what works best in your situation and within the responsibilities you have.

Associated Books

Breazeale, R., & Lumb, R. (2013). *Resilience Building: Peer Coaching*. ISBN-10: 1492812447 & ISBN-13: 978-1492812449. Amazon Publishing.

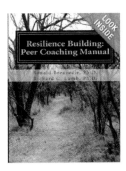

Lumb, R., & Rogers, J. (2013). *No Excuses Supervision: Role Changes to Reflect 21st Century Demands*. ISBN-10: 1493654373 & ISBN-13: 978-1493654376, Amazon Publishing.

A. Perceived Stress Self-Test[17]

The Perceived Stress Scale (PSS) is a classic stress assessment instrument. This tool, while originally developed in 1983, remains a popular choice for helping us understand how different situations affect our feelings and our perceived stress. It provides general indicators, not empirical certainty.

The questions in this scale ask about your feelings and thoughts during the last month. In each case, you will be asked to indicate how often you felt or thought a certain way. Although some of the questions are similar, there are differences between them and you should treat each one as a separate question. The best approach is to answer fairly quickly. That is, don't try to count up the number of times you felt a particular way; rather indicate the alternative that seems like a reasonable estimate.

---

[17]

http://faculty.weber.edu/molpin/healthclasses/1110/bookchapters/selfassessmentc hapter.htm

Self-Test

For each question choose from the following alternatives:

Place a check mark in the column box most representing your response to the question.

Self-assessment Question	0	1	2	3	4
1. In the last month, how often have you been upset because of something that happened unexpectedly?					
2. In the last month, how often have you felt that you were unable to control the important things in your life?					
3. In the last month, how often have you felt nervous and stressed?					
4. In the last month, how often have you felt confident about your ability to handle your personal problems?					
5. In the last month, how often have you felt that things were going your way?					
6. In the last month, how often have you found that you could not cope with all the things that you had to do?					
7. In the last month, how often have you been able to control irritations in your life?					
8. In the last month, how often have you felt that you were on top of things?					
9. In the last month, how often have you been angered because of things that happened that were outside of your control?					
10. In the last month, how often have you felt difficulties were piling up so high that you could not overcome them?					

Figuring your PSS score:

You can determine your PSS score by following these directions:

1. **First**, reverse your scores for questions **4, 5, 7,** & **8**. On these 4 questions, change the scores like this: **0 = 4, 1 = 3, 2 = 2, 3 = 1, 4 = 0**.

Nbr	Pg. 1 Original Score	Adjusted Score
1		
2		
3		
4		
5		
6		
7		
8		
9		
10		
TOT	**XXXXX**	

2. **Second,** add up your scores for each item to get a total. **My total score is _____.**

Individual scores on the PSS can range from 0 to 40 with higher scores indicating higher perceived stress.

Scores ranging from 0-13 would be considered **low** stress.
Scores ranging from 14-26 would be considered **moderate** stress.
Scores ranging from 27-40 would be considered **high** perceived stress.

Note: this is not a scientific test and the results are for self-awareness only.

Appreciation.

I wish to extend my appreciation to all of you who read and use this book in your leadership applications. I would sincerely welcome your comments and illustrations that apply to this books content. If you used this manuscript in ways that were helpful and found success, kindly send to me and your story will be included in subsequent revised editions.

Thank you,

Richard C. Lumb, Ph.D.
P.O. Box 852
Wilton, Maine 04294

Tele: 207-645-4924
Email: rclumb@gmail.com

CPSIA information can be obtained at www.ICGtesting.com
Printed in the USA
LVIW01n1422100118
562547LV00007B/83